Makes one want to revisit some of the stories studied in the past!

Reading this book and thinking of the struggles these people endured gave me even more appreciation for the forgiveness and tolerance God gives to us. The questions after each chapter were thought-provoking, as well.

Great book for Bible classes to study!

DEBBIE MAY, FORMER HCU
BOARD MEMBER

Bill and Laura Bagents are excellent writers. They have great skill in communicating biblical stories and the truths the stories teach. The focus of their writing, however, is not on their skill—though it is obviously there—but on the Word of God.

Wham! Facing Life's Heavy Hits is so well done. When you hurt, you must read this book, but there is more here than for simple reading. These good Bible students dive deeply into the lives of the Bible personalities they highlight.

Every time you read a chapter, you think, "Wow! That was great. That must be the best one," but the next is equally outstanding or even better.

The Story of each Old Testament person and his/her troubles is told in few words, yet it is all there. Caveats are given so that we can see the whole account even better. Care is given not to go too far. I appreciate the warning: "We're unwise to speculate or borrow trouble." Inferences come from the accounting of each wham, and the Implications are found and clearly given. Amidst the many blows of each Old Testament worthy, one wham is singled out for emphasis, and it always teaches us something we need to learn.

Do yourself a favor and study the Bible with this book. You will enjoy it.

ANDY KIZER, PULPIT MINISTER
OF SALEM CHURCH OF CHRIST,
FLORENCE, ALABAMA

WHAM! FACING LIFE'S HEAVY HITS

WHAM! FACING LIFE'S HEAVY HITS

THIRTEEN OLD TESTAMENT ENCOUNTERS

BILL BAGENTS

LAURA S. BAGENTS

CYPRESS

WHAM! Facing Life's Heavy Hits: Thirteen Old Testament Encounters

Copyright © 2022 by Bill Bagents and Laura S. Bagents

Published by Cypress Publications

Manufactured in the United States of America

Cataloging-in-Publication Data

Bagents, Bill (William Ronald), 1956-

WHAM! facing life's heavy hits: thirteen Old Testament encounters / Bill Bagents and Laura S. Bagents

p. cm.

ISBN 978-1-956811-25-4 (paperback) 978-1-956811-26-1 (ebook)

Library of Congress Control Number: 2022911809

1. Christian life. 2. Bible—Biography. I. Author. II. Bagents, Laura Lynn Stegall, 1960-. III. Title. IV. Series.

221.92—dc20

Cover design by Brittany Vander Maas and Laura S. Bagents.

This book is dedicated to everyone for whom these stories prove to be YOUR stories.

CONTENTS

Bible Abbreviations   xi

Introduction   xv

Wham 1: Adam and Eve   1
"We Did It to Ourselves"

Wham 2: Noah   8
A Damaged Legacy

Wham 3: Job   15
"I Just Want to Understand"

Wham 4: Abraham   23
Hope Delayed

Wham 5: Jacob   30
Self-Fulfilling Prophecies

Wham 6: Joseph   37
Sequential Setbacks

Wham 7: Moses   44
Life in a Pressure Cooker

Wham 8: Naomi   52
Lost Hope

Wham 9: David   59
Losing the Moral High Ground

Wham 10: Elijah   66
Pinnacle to Pit

Wham 11: Jeremiah   74
When All the World's Against You

Wham 12: Daniel   81
Stunning Disproportion

Wham 13: Esther   88
Illusion of Safety

Scripture Index   95
Acknowledgments   103
About the Authors   105
Also by Bill Bagents   107
Heritage Christian University Press   109

BIBLE ABBREVIATIONS

Old Testament

Gen	Genesis
Exod	Exodus
Lev	Leviticus
Num	Numbers
Deut	Deuteronomy
Josh	Joshua
Judg	Judges
Ruth	Ruth
1–2 Sam	1–2 Samuel
1–2 Kgs	1–2 Kings
1–2 Chr	1–2 Chronicles
Ezra	Ezra
Neh	Nehemiah
Esth	Esther
Job	Job
Ps	Psalms

Prov	Proverbs
Eccl	Ecclesiastes
Song	Song of Solomon
Isa	Isaiah
Jer	Jeremiah
Lam	Lamentations
Ezek	Ezekiel
Dan	Daniel
Hos	Hosea
Joel	Joel
Amos	Amos
Obad	Obadiah
Jonah	Jonah
Mic	Micah
Nah	Nahum
Hab	Habakkuk
Zeph	Zephaniah
Hag	Haggai
Zech	Zechariah
Mal	Malachi

New Testament

Matt	Matthew
Mark	Mark
Luke	Luke
John	John
Acts	Acts
Rom	Romans
1–2 Cor	1–2 Corinthians
Gal	Galatians
Eph	Ephesians
Phil	Philippians
Col	Colossians
1–2 Thess	1–2 Thessalonians
1–2 Tim	1–2 Timothy
Titus	Titus
Phlm	Philemon
Heb	Hebrews
Jas	James
1–2 Pet	1–2 Peter
1–2–3 John	1–2–3 John
Jude	Jude
Rev	Revelation

INTRODUCTION

From the creation, all that God made was good and very good (Gen 1:16, 31). But that didn't last long. As Genesis 3:1 implies, there had already been a spiritual disturbance—opposition to God existed even before humans sinned. Human sin just made evil more obvious and more personal. It also made human life more fragile and more challenging (Gen 3:16–19). It opened the door to life's whams, including both the consequences of sin and what Shakespeare poetically described as "the slings and arrows of outrageous fortune."

Just as God's blessings of sun, rain, and the beauties of nature bless both the evil and the just, the whams of life on a sin-damaged planet afflict everyone (Eccl 3:17–20). Sometimes personal sin is the cause, but often it's the sin of others that harms the innocent. Sometimes sin is causative only in the broadest of senses; it put people out of God's paradise and away from the protection of His overruling presence. Our earliest ancestors insisted on a degree of freedom from God, and their decision has cost us ever since. Some whams are foreseeable and preventable. Others come ambush-style, with neither warning nor recourse. They happen due to no fault of our own. Sometimes they happen without any hint of a reason.

We need to be careful with the phrase "with neither warning nor recourse." That statement isn't absolute. Scripture describes innumerable heavy hits afflicting people, both godly and not. Scripture warns us about the dangers, fragility, and uncertainties of life. And it offers more than just warning. It offers instruction and hope. No one helps us more than God in our hardest moments. And no one can match God's power to turn human struggles into spiritual victories—victories that help us love Him more as they equip us to bless our fellow strugglers.

We don't love the whams; we're not supposed to. But in our best moments, we can love what God does to us and through us as He helps us heal and learn.

Whams need not be joy-ending. They need not be life-defining. Some can be overcome, at least to a degree. Some we must incorporate into our story and service and endure until we reach the whamless and perfect peace of God. That's one of the greatest gifts of God: In Christ no blow, no matter how severe, will be allowed to harm us forever. Even in this life, it will not be allowed to harm us without purpose and meaning (Rom 8:28).

This book engages familiar Old Testament stories

through a narrow lens. For most of the stories, several life-altering whams will be listed, but the lens is a focus on one category of challenge or crisis. While we invite you to explore as broadly as you wish, we purposefully restrict our view for the sake of emphasis and practicality. We didn't want to create a 600-page book that would never be read. If the book were to be used in a Bible class setting, we wanted it to be reasonable for a one-quarter study. We tried to heed the paradoxical principle that less is sometimes more.

Disclaimer from Bill: I tend to battle most challenges with a degree of humor. For some readers, one or more of the life blows described in this book will be too recent and too traumatic for even the slightest levity to be appropriate. To you, I sincerely apologize. At any point you need to stop reading, bless yourself by doing just that. If it's ever right to resume, you will. Please know that I dare not make light of your pain. At the same time, please know that we want you to see God's light even through the darkest of pain.

WHAM 1: ADAM AND EVE
"WE DID IT TO OURSELVES"

THE STORY

We humans have an amazing history of failing to realize when we're blessed to the max. We think of Eden as ideal —perfect in climate, beauty, safety, and harmony. Spiritually-speaking, it was completely at peace in the most intimate presence of God. There was at least one rule: *"Of the tree of the knowledge of good and evil, you shall not eat" (Gen 2:17).* Yes, there was work; Adam was to tend the garden. And God blessed Adam with the job of naming the animals. But we view the work as easy, pleasant, rewarding, and fulfilling. Once Eve arrived, they were arguably (assuming an anticipation of children one day) as blessed as any couple could ever be. But somehow it wasn't enough.

The devil's cunning is a clinic in dark spiritual warfare (Gen 3). Offer no warning; raise no alarms. Don't scare the prey. Begin the conversation softly with a seemingly harmless question. Let the lady think she's in charge. Offer the false impression that you're only there to help or to learn. Don't take the humans on as a couple. If you can win one, the next conquest is likely to be easier. Tell the "safest" possible lie. Include as much truth as you can. Plant a seed of doubt. "Isn't there something God is withholding from you? How dare anything be withheld! You have the right to know what God knows and to make your own decisions."

The devil succeeded, and he still is. Question God's goodness, create doubt, and make sin look inviting. Make rebellion look like reaching for progress or asserting essential rights. Then, wait for the chips to fall.

THE WHAMS

The cascade of blows to Adam and Eve is stunning. Immediately, the first humans felt shame and exposure (Gen 3:7). Innocence and purity were gone. Then came fear of their Creator and a futile effort to hide from Him (Gen 3:18). There had been a HUGE negative change in their relationship to God. There was the clarity of knowing that their actions were both evil and indefensible. They had sinned against God and against themselves.

As the whams unfolded. Adam blamed Eve and he blamed God— *"the woman whom you gave to be with me ... ."* Though Scripture offers no comment, common sense invites thoughts of how husband blaming wife may have damaged their marriage. Add to that the stress of work becoming stunningly more difficult, pain being attached to childbirth, and at least a degree of change in the fundamental relationship of husband and wife (Gen 3:16). And Genesis 4 tells how the sin they introduced to humanity led to murder and banishment within their own family. In the actions of Cain, the first couple lost two sons. Their garden paradise was forever lost.

While the severity of the respective costs may be debated, this lesson chooses to emphasize the fact that Adam and Eve chose to disobey God. Their actions opened the door of pain and loss. Their sin made it easier for everyone who followed to choose sin. They did this to themselves, and that memory couldn't be erased.

IMPLICATIONS

A fierce question comes to mind. We imagine its being asked first as they left Eden, again when Abel died, and once more when Cain left them forever. "How could we have set this chain of events into motion?" The more common form of the question might be, "What were we thinking?" If they were spiritually minded, a better question would have been, "How could we do this to the God who created us?" That question leads to godly sorrow, repentance, and commitment to bear fruit worthy of repentance.

Another pertinent question: What should we learn from the life-changing blows to the first couple? Some scholars view the tight flow of Genesis 3:1–7 as indication that Adam was with Eve the whole time the serpent tempted her. If that's the case, the husband should never have been a passive observer. He should have acted to protect *"bone of his bones and flesh of his flesh."*

Adam and Eve should never have believed evil of God; neither should we. Anyone who in any way negatively questions the motives, character, or veracity of God must be viewed with extreme caution. The first couple did not have the benefit of James 1:13, but we do.

When faced with any temptation, the first key is recognition. The longer the devil can hide the hook, the better for him. The more quickly we identify the presence of an ungodly agenda, the faster we can implement an escape plan. Everyone who fights God loses—always. We have a tragic history of overestimating our awareness, intelligence, and understanding. It's so easy for us to think that we're in charge when we're being played (Prov 16:25 & 22:3, Rom 12:3, 1 Cor 10:12).

From the cascading whams that struck Adam and Eve, we can learn the avalanche power of sin. What looks harmless, often isn't. We all battle dark spiritual forces beyond both our vision and our comprehension (Eph 6:11–12). To employ an image from Greek mythology, once Pandora's Box is open, it may be impossible to close. A spark can start a fire that an army can't extinguish. It's like the neighbor from my youth who was going to save time and effort in lowering his pond by digging a tiny controllable trench at the top of the dam. Within moments, it was neither tiny nor controllable—the entire dam was lost.

Not all the implications are negative. God extended amazing mercy to Adam and Eve. He clothed them as they left the garden (Gen 3:21). When Cain was born, Eve recognized *"the help of the Lord"* (Gen 4:1). Genesis 4:25 speaks similarly of Seth's birth. Even murderous Cain received a mark of protection from God. The sin was punished, but the punishment was tempered by mercy.

CAVEATS

To their credit, Adam and Eve did not forget God. They didn't melt into apathy or unbelief. As their family grew, worship continued. As blessings came, they gave God glory. They worked. They survived. Even the wham of losing Eden and the level of intimacy they enjoyed with God before sin did not destroy them.

At this point we know many might welcome a discussion of human resilience, and we would not fault that as long as God was recognized as the source of that virtue. However, our hearts lean in a different direction. Perhaps to a degree, Adam and Eve stayed with God because they had no sensible option, but we suggest a more noble reason. We see Adam and Eve staying with God because God stayed with them. Even in the face of sin and judgment, He did too much that was too loving for them to doubt His righteous love.

No matter the depth of any terrible choice we make

and no matter the consequences that follow, we can still choose to stay with God. We accept the consequences. We work within the new reality. And we know that we're better off with God than without Him.

To expand on a statement from above: We humans have an amazing history of failing to realize when we're blessed to the max. In fairness to the first couple, ancient Israel didn't realize the rich blessing of having God as their king. They demanded a human leader like the nations around them (1 Sam 8). Like his father, Solomon didn't recognize the blessing of God's plan for marriage (Gen 2:24), so he multiplied wives like the pagan kings (1 Kgs 11:3–4). Hezekiah couldn't be satisfied with the number of years God gave him and pled for longer life (Isa 38, 2 Kgs 20–21)—a decision that led to the birth and reign of evil Manasseh and paved the way for the Babylonian invasion. Extending to Jesus's time on earth, His people refused to welcome a spiritual kingdom and rejected the greatest gift that God could ever offer (John 1:1–13). And people can still repeat that horrible decision (Heb 3:12–19 & 6:4–8, 2 Pet 2:18–22, Rev 2:4–5). All who play with sin find themselves played by sin. The player always becomes the prey.

QUESTIONS FOR DISCUSSION

1. What does the serpent's success in temptation tell us about sin and Satan?

2. What does the serpent's success in temptation tell us about humans?
3. Do you picture Adam and Eve grieving the loss of Eden? If so, describe your image of their grief.
4. Playing devil's advocate, how would you have tempted Adam and Eve to give up on God after their banishment from Eden?
5. How do you picture Adam comforting Eve after their sin and banishment (for men)? For ladies, how do you picture Eve comforting Adam?

WHAM 2: NOAH
A DAMAGED LEGACY

THE STORY

Precious few people had as direct a role in the preservation of humanity as Noah. On the pivot points of *"My spirit shall not abide in man forever" (Gen 6:3),* *"every intention of his heart was only evil continually ..." (Gen 6:5),* *"and the Lord regretted that he had made man on the earth" (Gen 6:6),* *"Noah found grace in the eyes of the Lord" (Gen 6:8).*

Genesis 6:9 describes Noah as a righteous and blameless man who walked with God. Though he lived in an utterly corrupt world, Noah solidified his excellent reputation by continuing to do all that God commanded him (Gen 6:22). To the best of our knowledge, he built the ark in a world that had never known rain or flood. He took God at His word with never a record of complaint. And his first recorded action upon leaving the ark was to build an altar and offer sacrifices to God (Gen 8:20). That act of worship is reported immediately before God promised never to destroy the earth by flood again (Gen 8:21–23).

Praise of Noah isn't limited to the book of Genesis. Ezekiel 14:12–20 cites Noah, Daniel, and Job as men counted righteous by God. Hebrews 11:7 reminds us that Noah was a man of faith who *"became an heir of the righteousness that comes by faith."* 2 Peter 2:5 describes Noah as *"a herald of righteousness"* who was preserved by God.

While we continue to be grateful for this outstanding man, Scripture offers us a chilling reminder that he was just as human as the rest of us. Genesis 9:20–27 reports a sordid set of events that stained Noah's legacy. He planted a vineyard, drank the wine, and lay uncovered in his tent. This led to inappropriate conduct by his son Ham and a stout curse of servitude by Noah upon Ham's son Canaan.

Genesis 9:20–27 is brief and challenging. We don't know why the grandson rather than the son was cursed. It's likely that cultural expectations were in play that are lost to us. It seems obvious that more happened than the Holy Spirit chose to report. The Bible has an amazing record of being clear and plainspoken without drifting into titillation or lewdness. Lore and speculation abound, but neither carries real weight, certainly not the weight of Scripture. This much we know: Noah should not have been drunk. By being drunk, he put his family and himself at spiritual risk. He opened doors for loss and conflict that should never have been opened.

THE WHAMS

How would you describe the whams of Genesis 9:20–27? Getting drunk when the Bible so frequently and stoutly condemns drunkenness certainly qualifies. While the condemnatory texts were written long after Noah's day, we see it as virtually certain that God's oral warnings preceded the written ones (Prov 20:1 & 23:29–35, Gal 5:21). Noah was drunk to the point that he did not know what had happened to him and surrounding him until after the fact (Gen 9:24).

Though we would not argue that nakedness is always sinful, clearly something was wrong with Noah's conduct within his tent during this disappointing episode. Shem and Japheth are presented positively for choosing not even to view what Ham had described to them.

Ham's conduct is not presented positively. The text implies at least two reasons. He did not act to minimize the damage of this episode, and he reported it to his brothers. Reporting rather than correcting opens the door to thoughts of gossip and disrespect.

It would be difficult to doubt that Noah lost respect in the eyes of his family. It's possible that he did additional damage by cursing his grandson. The Bible accurately reports what Noah said, but it does not tell us whether his words were wise, fair, or excessive.

While we'd never assert that Noah was sinless before this event, we noted above that Scripture describes him as both righteous and blameless. In a world ruled by sin, his moral record to date was sufficient to attract God's grace and blessing. There is no record of family discord. The Bible's presentation of his life is stellar. That brings us to the wham emphasized in this chapter—as an older and previously exemplary servant of God, Noah damaged his legacy through one sad episode.

IMPLICATIONS

Pre-flood, the devil didn't own Noah. In a totally debased world, Noah held on to God and righteousness. He and the Creator remained on solid speaking terms. Through the events of Genesis 9:20–27, Satan controlled Noah—at least for a time. A clear implication is that Satan never gives up. Even after utterly failing with Jesus in the wilderness, we're told *"he departed from him until an opportune time" (Luke 4:13)*. No wonder we're urged to be sober-minded and watchful (1 Pet 5:8)! We can imagine the devil's wanting our allegiance early in life so he can maximize the harm that we do. In Noah's case (as with Solomon and Hezekiah), we can see him delighting in a late-in-life fall.

Noah's choice to make intoxicating wine reminds us of Satan's power to corrupt virtually any aspect of God's creation. Food can be turned into an instrument of power and punishment. In rich societies it can become an idol of excess. So in Genesis 9, a wholesome, handsome, and healthy creation of God was morphed (twisted, corrupted) into a mind-numbing and morality-suppressing tool of sin.

The sad episode of Noah's drunkenness also reminds us that we can't always count on our families to make good decisions. Shem and Japheth did, but Ham and (in some way unknown to us) Canaan did not. We lack many details—but Noah, who was there, judged them guilty and said so! And God chose to record his words for us.

An enormous implication revolves around the effect of this sin on Noah's family. We don't know how much it changed the relation of Shem, Ham, and Japheth. We don't know what percentage of the ongoing conflict between the Canaanites and Israel originated in Noah's curse from Genesis 9. We think of James 3:5: *"How great a forest is set ablaze by such a small fire!"* Since we can't know all the damage that could come, we're wise not to strike sin's match.

Of similar magnitude is the powerful reminder to avoid deifying any human. Even as the man who played a stunning role in the survival of humanity, Noah was still just a man. God alone is worthy of worship and absolute trust (Deut 6:4–5 & 6:13, quoted by Jesus in Matt 4:10).

Might we summarize a huge implication in the more modern proverb, "There's no fool like an old fool"? If we read Genesis 9:28 correctly at the time of this sin, Noah was somewhere in the final 350 years of his 950-year-life. The families who reared us would unite to say, "Clearly old enough to know better." Did he fall victim to the delusion of personal exceptionalism? "I know what intoxicants do, but it won't treat me that badly if I do it just this once." Did he rationalize? "I've been such a good person for such a log time. Surely, I'm entitled to go my own way just this once." While we can't read Noah's mind, we are wise to consider what could have happened so we don't repeat his sin.

The key implication for the theme of this lesson stands clear. As long as there's breath and life, Satan still seeks to destroy. Not even 600 years of faithfulness made Noah immune. We're not immune either. Like Noah, we will come to the end of our days. Unless the Lord returns first, we will die. And we want to leave this world faithful in the Lord.

CAVEATS

Some might read this lesson and think, "How sad that these authors think Noah is forever lost due to a single sin." We've emphasized the gravity of this specific sin, but we meet Noah in Scripture after Genesis 9. From the positive words of Ezekiel 14, Hebrews 11, and 1 Peter 5, we're happy to say that we expect to meet Noah in heaven. We love and never diminish the power of God's grace.

It would also be unfortunate if we led you to believe that Noah's sin robbed him of all future spiritual influence within his family. If only the sinless could influence their families for good, Romans 3:23 disqualifies us all. Sin so often does far more harm that we could ever foresee, so we never play with it. But those who turn from sin and resume their walk with God send an amazingly powerful message. From Noah, we're reminded that a damaged legacy is not a destroyed legacy.

QUESTIONS FOR DISCUSSION

1. Why would the Bible include this embarrassing episode from the life of a man who served God with such amazing faithfulness?

2. Sometimes people offer excuses for Noah's winemaking and drunkenness. "He didn't know it was intoxicating. He'd never seen people get drunk before." Why would anyone offer excuse? Why doesn't the Bible ever offer excuse for sin?

3. How can we explain the radically different levels of respect paid to Noah by Shem and Japheth versus Ham?

4. We would never claim that Noah intended for his sin to harm his family. What, if anything, does lack of intent to harm have to do with actual harm?

5. What is your best understanding of Noah's legacy? How would God have us think of Noah?

WHAM 3: JOB
"I JUST WANT TO UNDERSTAND"

THE STORY

Few biblical stories are as familiar—and as misunderstood—as the life of Job. This blameless, upright, God-fearing, and good man was also stunningly blessed. There were seven sons, three daughters, flocks, herds, servants, friends, health, and respect. Scripture says of him, *"This man was the greatest of all the people of the east" (Job 1:1–3).* And he lost it all in a horrific onslaught by Satan.

Between a brief introduction and an amazing conclusion, the bulk of the book of Job records efforts by Job's friends to get him to acknowledge that his losses were his fault. Surely, Job had some huge but hidden sin. They asked him rhetorically, *"Who that was innocent ever perished? Or where were the upright cut off?" (Job 4:7)*

Working from that false assumption, they hammered Job without mercy.

Most of the book of Job is the darkest of tragedy. As Job battled fierce grief, his well-meaning friends urged him to confess and turn from the sin that had caused his calamity. As Job lamented his birth (Job 3) and vividly described his pain (Job 6), he could not do as his "friends" requested. He could not because he knew that he hadn't broken faith with God. He begged his friends to prove otherwise (Job 6:24–30). But they never did.

Since his friends couldn't explain what was happening to him, Job turned his words toward God.

> *Today also my complaint is bitter; my hand is heavy on account of my groaning. Oh, that I might know where I might find him, that I might come even to his seat. I would lay my case before him and fill my mouth with arguments. I would know what he would answer me and understand what he would say to me ... There an upright man could argue with him, and I would be acquitted forever by my judge (Job 23:2–7)."*

Job's words grew even stouter. *"I cry out to you for help, and you do not answer me; I stand, and you only look at me. You have turned cruel to me; with the might of your hand you persecute me"* (Job 30:20–21). Finally, the Lord speaks, and

Job backs away from his pained but ignorant words (Job 38:1–42:6).

THE WHAMS

The economic losses were devastating. All the flocks, all the herds, and the bulk of the servants were gone (Job 1:13–17).

As severe as those losses were, they could not hold a candle to the loss of all ten of his children in a single calamity (Job 3:18–19). Even in that crisis, *"Job did not sin or charge the Lord with wrong" (Job 1:22).*

But the tragedy was not over. Satan *"struck Job with loathsome sores from the sole of his foot to the crown of his head" (Job 2:7).* The situation was so dire, that Job's wife offered the infamous recommendation, *"Curse God and die" (Job 2:9).*

Job experienced public ridicule during his trials (Job 30:9–15). The broader community failed to observe the healthy proverb: "You don't kick a man when he's down." It's like they took joy in the fall of the once strong and favored Job. How cruel!

At least it appeared that Job still had his oldest, and presumably wisest, friends. Initially, they did great. They came to offer sympathy and comfort. They sat with him for seven full days before speaking a word (Job 2:11–13). And then, as noted above, his "friends" became his attackers. It was numerically unfair, three on one. It was unfair in terms of their certainty and unwillingness to listen. It was unfair in terms of the way they escalated and personalized their attacks.

As terrible as everything listed above was, all of it combined was not what most troubled Job. The blow that most afflicted Job was having no clue why it happened, not having even a single word from the Lord.

IMPLICATIONS

Job offers clear proof that no one is immune from Satan's attacks. Some have reasoned poorly and asked, "Why did God paint a target on Job's back by mentioning him to Satan?" (Job 1:8) Do they really think that Satan had never noticed Job before that moment? How odd an assumption! It doesn't fit with 1 Peter 5:8. The devil is stunningly aware of every faithful servant of God.

Job offers an impressive reminder of the fragility of the human condition. People whom we love die unexpectedly. Health fails. The things that we enjoy can be taken in a moment. We're so blessed that *"one's life does not consist in the abundance of his possessions" (Luke 12:15b)*.

Job reminds us that life-long friends can be passionate, well-intentioned, and tragically wrong. We all have blind spots, including unwarranted assumptions. We so need to stay submissive to God's truth, to be willing to learn God's truth *"more accurately" (Acts 18:26)*.

Job also reminds us of the damaging effect of hammering pressure even on the strongest of believers. Note the contrast between Job 1:22 and 30:20–21. While we would assert that Job kept his vow not to stop trusting God (Job 13:15), Job clearly said more than he should have about "God's actions." To the best of our knowledge, Job never knew that every attack he faced came from the devil. In his worst moment, he accused the Lord of cruelty and persecution. In his best moment, he humbly repented and found God stunningly gracious (Job 42). God even vindicated Job before his friends.

Our point of emphasis within this story of tragedy, trial, and triumph is its massive wham to Job's heart, mind, and faith. What was happening to him made no sense. It ran counter to all that he knew and believed. How could a person who tried so hard to live for God lose everything in dramatic and cascading fashion? Job had not broken faith with God. How could this be happening to him? And his emphasis time after time was simply, "I just want to understand. If God would just tell me why, I could bear this. I need for this to make sense."

Ironically, God never explained to Job. To the best of our knowledge, He never told Job about Satan's challenge. He never answered the question, "Why do bad (immeasurably tragic) things happen to good people?" God did not withhold explanation because He was unable to explain. Based on our two lifetimes of experience and loads of help from people wiser than we are, our thoughts go in a different direction. God didn't explain to Job because neither Job nor any other human would be capable of understanding.

Considerable biblical evidence can be offered in support of this belief. Isaiah 55:8–9 reads,

> *For my thoughts are not your thoughts,*
> *neither are your ways my ways, declares*
> *the Lord.*
> *For as the heavens are higher than the earth,*
> *so are my ways higher than your ways and*
> *my thoughts than your thoughts."*

Paul echoes these words in Romans 11:32–33.

> *Oh, the depth of the riches and wisdom and*
> *knowledge of God! How unsearchable are*
> *His judgments and how inscrutable are*
> *his ways! For who has known the mind of*
> *the Lord, or who has been His counselor?"*

Even those who walked with Jesus daily for some three years were not able to "bear" [grasp, deal with, understand] all that He needed to tell them at the end of His earthly ministry (John 16:12–13). There are countless realities and complexities that exceed human capacity.

What are we to do in those moments when life doesn't make sense? Job offers powerful counsel. We hold on to God anyway. *"Though he slay me, I will hope in him ..."* *(Job 13:15a).* There is no feasible or inviting alternative. And there's also no way to say how challenging hoping in

God becomes when life as we've known it crashes around us.

The bottom line to Job's spiritual survival is amazing. It didn't come through getting the answers he wanted. Neither did it come from being allowed to ask all his challenging questions. It didn't come from strength of will or character. Rather, it came from grasping more of the greatness of God. It came from God's gracious self-revelation and Job's willingness to humble himself under the mighty hand of God (Jas 4:10).

CAVEATS

If we were to think of Job as a hero of the faith who never struggled and perfectly handled unthinkable calamity, we'd be horribly mistaken. While heroic in many respects, he struggled with every fiber of his being. And God was with him far more than he realized during the depths of his pain.

Job said more to and about God than was wise. But when he was given opportunity to step back and listen to the Lord, he took it. Job came to the realization that many never reach: "It's not about me. I exist by the grace—and for the glory—of God. God owes me no answers."

We can't know Job's perspective on the loss of his first ten children. While we have no doubt that he missed them every day, we have great hope that he thought of them as safe with the Lord. We'd never argue that Job's second ten children could replace the first ten. Life and hearts don't work like that. But at the end of his story, Job is more blessed than in the beginning (Job 42:12). He enjoyed four generations of family. And when he died, *"an old man, and full of days" (Job 42:17),* the best of his blessings began—never another loss or struggle in God's perfect tomorrow.

QUESTIONS FOR DISCUSSION

1. Of all the losses Job endured, which do you view as the biggest blow? Why?
2. Why did the Lord allow Satan to deal so fiercely with Job?
3. Why were Job's friends so certain that some secret sin had led to his losses?
4. What does the friends' certainty tell us about the nature, limits, and dangers of human understanding?
5. Why do so many people still believe that "if only I could know the reason, I could do better at facing life's biggest losses"? What makes this belief dangerous?

WHAM 4: ABRAHAM
HOPE DELAYED

THE STORY

As we meet Abram (before his famous name change), we encounter several major characteristics of Hebrew storytelling. From Genesis 11:27 onward, there's notable repetition of key ideas. There's foreshadowing: *"Now Sarai was barren; she had no child" (Gen 11:30).* Numerous family members are mentioned, setting up the contrast with Genesis 12:1, *"Now the Lord said to Abram, 'Go from your country and your kindred and your father's house ... .'"* The report of Sarai's childlessness stands in stark contrast to God's promise: *"And I will make of you a great nation ... ."* Nephew Lot is mentioned, preparing us to expect to see him again.

Abram was 75 as he left Haran (Gen 12:4), helping us to understand that he and Sarai journeyed with God for 25 years before the birth of their son, Isaac (Gen 21:5).

Twenty-five years on a dangerous journey without a map and without an heir. Though the heir came in God's good time, Abraham experienced delayed hope in a second major sense. In describing the faithfulness of the patriarchs and matriarchs, Hebrews 11:13 beautifully reminds us, *"These all died in faith, not having received the things promised, but having seen them and greeted them from afar, and having acknowledged that they were strangers and exiles on the earth."*

Such was the power of their faith. They took God at His word, serving and growing in faith as God advanced His plan at His pace.

THE WHAMS

For some, being told to leave kin and country would have been a major wham. We can't be certain of Abram's outlook or emotions—we know only what Scripture tells us. For many of us, distance from family would cause major damage to our support system.

For others, there'd be a wham in being sent on a journey with neither map nor destination. But we must acknowledge that some would find that to be a fine adventure. We have friends who leave on vacation (yes, a much different situation that Abram's) without having chosen the place or nature of their travel.

We would not want to miss the fact that Abram and Sarai's journey began after the death of his father (Gen 11:32). The standard life coach advice is, "Don't make a major decision within a year of a major loss." While that's not Scripture, it is time-honored and leans toward safety.

Abram and Sarai encountered other whams. Genesis 12 records a famine, a trip to Egypt for survival, and danger posed by Sarai's beauty. Genesis 20 recounts a very similar story involving a side-trip to Gerar.

There's the infamous set of conflicts and crises connected to Lot. Servants of Abram and Lot clashed over growing herds and limited resources (Gen 13:1–13). Lot's moving to Sodom led to the need for an armed rescue (Gen 14).

On top of those struggles is the self-inflicted wham of choosing to have a child with Sarai's servant, Hagar (Gen 16). It created anger and envy in Sarai's heart and led to Hagar and Ishmael twice leaving Abram's group (Gen 20). Though the plot was Sarai's, she demanded that Abram send his son and Hagar away, a matter that was most displeasing to Abram (Gen 20:10–11).

The conflict emphasized in this lesson is the daily and cumulative pain of childlessness for 25 years. It is empha-sized numerous times, including the episode with Hagar. It's painfully brought to bear when the Lord reminds Abram that his descendants will be uncountable, *"like the dust of the earth" (Gen 13:16)*. The promise is repeated in Genesis 15 and in association with his name change in Genesis 17. The delay is emphasized as Sarah passed the age of childbearing (Gen 18:11). The text is purposefully obvious; God did not grant Sarah a son until it was physi-cally impossible for her to conceive (Gen 21).

IMPLICATIONS

As teachers have noted for centuries, God does not "do time" like people do. As an eternal being, He lives beyond time. Famously, *"with the Lord one day is as a thousand years and a thousand years as one day. The Lord is not slow to fulfill his promise as some men count slowness" (2 Pet 3:8–9).* Consider the centuries between the earliest hint of the birth of Jesus (Gen 3:15) and the birth of the Christ *"in the fullness of time" (Gal 4:4).*

Abraham's faithfulness clearly documents faith's power to persevere across years. We make no claim that this perseverance is easy—just that it's possible. In itself, that's a huge spiritual benefit. Think of Noah, Joseph, Daniel, as well as Anna and Simeon from Luke 2.

Abraham powerfully reminds us that our spiritual journeys are not straight-line. He faced fear, famine, conflict, family discord, and doubt. But God never gave up on him. The Lord employed the strangest of means to grow Abraham's faith. Who but the Lord would have dreamed that the covenant of circumcision, instituted a year before Isaac's birth, could serve as evidence of His covenant (Gen 17)? Who but the Lord would have the patience to allow both Abraham and Sarah to laugh at His promise without offense (Gen 17:17 & 18:11–15)? Who but the Lord would be able to overcome a series of lies as weak faith needed to grow (Gen 12:10–13, 18:15 & 20:1–13)? Who but the Lord could so effectively use both the faith and the failings of Abrahan and Sarah to bless, warn, and encourage us?

Hope delayed turns our thoughts to Romans 5:1–5. The core of that passage deals with the formative power of faith during trials.

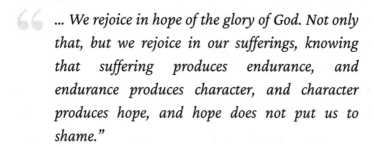

> *... We rejoice in hope of the glory of God. Not only that, but we rejoice in our sufferings, knowing that suffering produces endurance, and endurance produces character, and character produces hope, and hope does not put us to shame."*

CAVEATS

A danger in studying about biblical people, especially heroes, is the false assumption that they knew the outcome of their trials and journeys from the start. In truth, they walked by faith like we do, and faith is not sight. There's great loss in thinking that people like Abraham knew all the outcomes in advance and were forewarned of every trial. May the Lord help us avoid reading poor assumptions into the text.

This lesson is written primarily from Abraham's perspective. He is much more prominent within Scripture. However, Sarah's perspective and faithfulness also matter. She merits positive mention in both Hebrews 11 and 1 Peter 3. It is our observation that Sarah's laughing at God's promise gets remembered far more often—and more nega-tively—than Abraham's. We wonder why. It's possible that many are too hard on Sarah for her plan to "help God" through Hagar. While her actions were desperate and proved foolish, they may well have been accepted within her culture. Think of Jacob fathering children with both his wives and their servants. We're so thankful that God doesn't judge us based only on our worst moments.

God invented family. No one is more pro-family than God. Some have found it surprising that part of God's call to Abram was to leave both his country and his kindred. We'd never view that as an anti-family action, especially knowing that Abraham sent his servant back to Nahor in Mesopotamia, back to his people, to find a wife for Isaac (Gen 24:1–10). We're reminded that sometimes what looks like a wham isn't. We've all seen people mature impressively as they "left father and mother" and stood with God as their own family unit. Certainly, Abraham grew into an impressive spiritual leader when God put him in a position where that was essential.

While Abraham's mandate to sacrifice Isaac as a burnt offering to God (Gen 22) is not central to this lesson, it's one of Scripture's most surprising stories. Elsewhere God utterly condemns child sacrifice as an abomination punishable by death (Lev 18:21 & 20:1–5, Deut 12:31, Jer 19:5 & 32:35, 2 Kgs 23:10). Genesis 22 seems so out of character with the flow of Scripture and the nature of the Almighty. Three words of caution: God stopped the process; Isaac was not killed. Secondly, this event wonderfully encourages humility; if we ever think that we have reached a full understanding of God, we need to rediscover our ignorance and repent. Finally, we see the fruit of Abraham's spiritual growth. He doesn't know just how, *"but God will provide for himself the lamb" (Gen 22:6)*. Even if Isaac was the lamb, Abraham *"considered that he was able even to raise him from the dead" (Heb 11:19)*. One way or another, God would be right and do right.

QUESTIONS FOR DISCUSSION

1. Why would God choose to give His promise to Abram knowing that the fulfillment would be 25 years in the future?
2. What do the struggles that God let faithful Abraham endure tell us about the nature of God? The nature of humans?
3. Other than the wham of waiting 25 years for a son, what do you see as the greatest crisis that Abraham and Sarah faced?
4. After all the previous challenges, why would God give Abraham the final test of commanding him to sacrifice Isaac?
5. What enabled Abraham to pass that final test?

WHAM 5: JACOB

SELF-FULFILLING PROPHECIES

THE STORY

Is there a more conflicted and confusing person in all of Scripture than Jacob? He was a mamma's boy who was not afraid to manipulate his he-man twin (Gen 25). He pulled off one of the most ruthless deceptions recorded in the Bible—he borrowed clothes, wrapped himself in the skin of a goat, and lied to his old, blind father to steal the birthright blessing (Gen 27).

He was blessed with the vision of a ladder to heaven with angels ascending and descending (Gen 28:10–17). He learned from Uncle Laban that even cons can be conned (Gen 29:15–30). He wrestled with an angel and got both a damaged hip and a blessing from that encounter (Gen 32:13–32). Though Jacob had the audacity to demand a blessing from an angel, he dreaded his "reunion" with Esau. He led his family, but not always—as Rachel's theft of her father's idol (Gen 31:34) and the slaughter of the men of Shechem show (Gen 34).

Though he knew first-hand the dangers of parental favoritism, he repeated that bad family pattern with his son Joseph (Gen 37:3). In a way, he also repeated the pattern by loving second wife Rachel more than first wife Leah (Gen 29). He tripled the error by preferring Benjamin after Joseph was gone.

Jacob lived many of his latter years in inconsolable grief over the assumed death of the beloved Joseph (Gen 37:29–36). He endured famine and a move to Egypt. He died in a foreign land with a request that his bones be returned home for burial (Gen 50:5).

THE WHAMS

There's no way Jacob could have known the currents he created when he enticed Esau to sell his birthright (Gen 25:29–34), but he had to know on some level that this was not a brotherly act. The text doesn't describe Jacob's mindset or the process he used to concoct this plan, but it hardly seems spur-of-the-moment. The supplanter is living down to his name, seemingly without thought of the resulting family rifts.

The sale of the birthright would have meant nothing without the accompanying patriarchal blessing. And Jacob acquired that blessing by hook and crook with the aid of his mother (Gen 27). Though she willingly helped him, for the rest of her days Rebekah would live with the disrespect she showed Isaac and the pain she caused her firstborn. For the rest of his days, Jacob would live with the consequences of his lie.

Esau's skill as a hunter gave teeth to his hatred of Jacob (Gen 27:41). Ironically, Esau showed more respect for Isaac than both Rebekah and Jacob. At least he was willing to delay his vengeance until his father's death. The wham of Esau's vengeful plan was exile. Jacob had to run. Not only did he spend years away from his family of birth, he had to face the dread of eventually seeing Esau again.

The wham of Jacob's being fooled by Laban is classic and comical—the player gets played (Gen 29:13–30). Not only was he played, he got played by a relative at the cost of seven years' labor, a wife he never wanted, and a permanently conflicted family system. The world would say "karma," but we think of sowing and reaping (Gal 6:7–8) and God's immutable law that sin can't be hidden (Num 32:23).

Of course Jacob wasn't "played" only once. As mentioned above, his adult sons envied and hated their brother. They sold Joseph into slavery and used his famous tunic to deceive Jacob into thinking that he was dead (Gen 37:29–36). When this conspiracy of lies was finally brought to light, did Jacob in any way link it to the way he had deceived Esau? Did he ever see this as fruit from seed that he planted?

Like Adam and Eve, it's a case of "I did this to myself." More specifically, Jacob had multiple opportunities to see

This episode left Jacob with the blessing of a new name—Israel (contends with God, Prince of God)—and a permanent limp. Was the limp another wham, or was it more? Through all his days, God had blessed Jacob far more than he realized. And God was about to bless him again through a peaceful reunion with Esau. Through all his days, Jacob had limped along, never quite sure how much to rely on the Lord (Gen 28:20–22). In many senses, Jacob's story is ours. It's amazing what God can do with, for, and through us when we welcome Him. It's tragic how much we can get in God's way when we try to run life without Him.

CAVEATS

We have heard severe and scary "backwards reasoning" within studies of the life of Jacob. Based on the prophecy recorded in Genesis 25:19–26, some have proposed that Jacob's poor treatment of Esau and securing the birthright through deception are somehow non-sinful because they moved God's plan forward. We need great caution here! God never sins and never tempts anyone to sin (Jas 1:12–16). When God offered this predictive prophecy, He accurately foretold what was going to happen, but He neither stated nor ordained the details. In God's greatness, there could have been many—and far more honorable—paths for the younger son to lead and advance. God's prophecy did not lock Jacob into evil actions.

himself reaping what he had sown. He lived in a ch
lenging cycle of his own creation that he could neitl
control nor end.

IMPLICATIONS

We humans are never half as clever as we think we are.
When we hatch plots for our advancement without
seeking God's blessing and guidance, we're in terribly
dangerous territory. We're unknowingly inviting future
whams. When we hatch plots that violate God's nature
and God's law, we cross into sin and risk earning sin's
ultimate wages (Rom 6:23).

The life of Jacob begs us to ask ourselves, "Who's
more able to take care of me—God or I? Who has the
better record of success? Who has the most knowledge?
The most wisdom? The most power? The most resources?
Who's more likely to get this right?"

As hinted above, when we choose a less than honorable path, we have no way to foresee all the lives that will
be impacted. Rebekah became complicit in Jacob's
conspiracy. Though Esau bore responsibility for despising
his birthright (Gen 25:34), Jacob tempted him to do so.
Jacob made it easier for his brother to choose wrong over
right.

Genesis 32:22–32 describes Jacob wrestling with "a
man" whom he believed to be more than a man ("*I have
seen God face to face, and yet my life has been preserved*"). In
many ways, Jacob had been wrestling with God all his life.

"Self-fulfilling prophecies" is not a biblical phrase, but we believe it to be a biblical concept. Our actions, assumptions, and attitudes shape us. A major reason to avoid sinful thinking is that sinful thinking leads to sinful actions. Our mindset matters (Col 3:1). Our outlook maters (Phil 4:8). We have the God-given ability to *"think with sober judgment"* and to *"be transformed by the renewal of [our] minds" (Rom 12:2)*. But every step away from God makes those good practices less likely and more difficult. That's one of the key reasons that *"the way of the transgressor is difficult" (Prov 13:15 NKJV, Hos 14:9)*.

On a common sense level, a child who is constantly called worthless and dumb usually lives down to those words. A person who believes himself to be helpless tends to act helplessly. People who tell themselves "I can't get ahead," seldom do. And Christians who believe themselves to be made in the image of God, redeemed by the blood of Jesus, and loved by our Savior, have every reason to live up to that high calling.

QUESTIONS FOR DISCUSSION

1. In what ways does God help us by recording the prophecy of Genesis 25:23? What lessons can be drawn from that passage?
2. If Jacob and Esau knew about this prophecy, how could that have affected their lives?

3. Does this lesson overplay the idea of self-fulfilling prophecy? If so, in what ways?

4. Consider the statement, "Jacob's story [of wrestling with God] is ours." In what senses is it accurate? Helpful? Dangerous?

5. In what ways do you find Jacob's life story to be encouraging—particularly in terms of how God treated him?

WHAM 6: JOSEPH

SEQUENTIAL SETBACKS

THE STORY

We must be careful not to transport modern western concepts of adolescence back to the ancient near east, but we meet Joseph at age 17 (Gen 37:2). He was the favorite son of a famous father, and he had the multi-colored tunic to prove it. Did his dad ever recognize the target that he put on Joseph's back?

It's difficult to know which is worse, the tunic or the dreams. Joseph's brothers hated the dreams, and his father wasn't approving either (Gen 37:5–11). The brothers would not speak peaceably to him (Gen 37:4), eventually planning his murder. Through Reuben's intervention and God's providence, they settled on selling him to Ishmaelite slavers (Gen 37:18–28).

As a slave in Egypt, Joseph excelled until a lie put him in prison (Gen 39). He excelled in prison, but endured an extra two years of confinement because a man whom he had helped forgot his promise (Gen 40:1–41:1).

When rescued from prison to interpret Pharaoh's dream, Joseph was elevated to second-in-command in Egypt. He married, was blessed with children, and led a grain production and storage effort that saved countless lives. Life was good until he found himself face to face with the brothers who betrayed him (Gen 42). At that point, he put it all together; he came to realize the meaning of his dreams and his role in God's plan (Gen 42:9). And he faced perhaps the greatest challenge of his life.

THE WHAMS

At age 17 can we blame a boy (young man?) for sharing his strange dreams? Would his brothers have been kinder about the dreams if Jacob had not set Joseph up to be hated? His dad didn't know what to do with him, and his brothers wanted nothing to do with him. In some ways, Joseph had lost his family even before the slavers took him away.

How do we imagine the blow of transitioning from favored son of a rich man to household slave in a foreign land? Joseph made that transition and held on to his faith only to be falsely accused of a sin he refused to commit out of loyalty to God (Gen 39:9). While we don't at all like the statement, Joseph looks like the poster boy for "no good deed goes unpunished."

House slave in a foreign land can't be a great situation, but it has to be better than prison. And Joseph found himself a young foreign prisoner accused of a sexual crime. There's no way to expect news from home—how is his aging father? There's injustice upon injustice, compounded by the two-year forgetfulness of Pharaoh's chief cupbearer.

And after his deliverance, when life finally seemed to be in order, his evil brothers came to town for grain. The text implies that he had put the pain of the past behind him. He named his first son Manasseh, *"God has made me forget all my hardship and my father's house" (Gen 41:51)*. The second boy was Ephraim, *"God has made me fruitful in the land of my affliction" (Gen 41:52)*. After some seven years of peace, old wounds were suddenly ripped open.

Even after forgiving his brothers, saving their lives, and helping the whole family move to Egypt, Joseph endured the wham of his brothers doubting his forgiveness. We don't know if their fears flowed from their guilt or their character, but they said, *"It may be that Joseph will hate us and pay us back for all the evil that we did to him" (Gen 50:15)*. And Joseph had to forgive them one more time.

IMPLICATIONS

In some ways, Joseph's life is a mini version of Job's. A key difference is that while Job's losses came at whirlwind speed, Joseph's were more spread over time. He had "opportunity" for maximum pain and reflection. It seems unwise to speculate about which situation was worse. Such stunning whams are fierce blows to mind and heart. Fierce is always fierce.

There's no biblical hint that Joseph asked the Hebrew version of "What's a guy got to do to catch a break?" If he was a man of few words, he could have simply asked, "Again?" We know the Bible is brief and doesn't report every thought, but we love to think of Joseph not wasting time and effort on moot points. We love to think of him using all his faith to keep serving God.

In many respects, "Again?" is the question people keep asking. We assume a happy, blessed childhood filled with accomplishments and great memories. Young adulthood moves into enjoying friends and establishing a career. And it's hard for us to remember how affluent and Western those assumptions are. Most of the world struggles more like Joseph.

Joseph seems to have lived by the motto "do the next right thing." To his everlasting credit, he let God define "right." Joseph never played the victim. To the best of our knowledge, he never (falsely) declared himself unable to obey God or exempt from God's standards. He never claimed that extreme circumstances suspend God's commands. There's no hint of "Just this once, I have to look out for myself. Making the moral decision could get me hurt."

We think of Joseph giving superior answers to crucial questions. "How many times am I going to have to choose

God's way over what's easy?" As many as it takes. "How many times is Satan going to attack me?" As many as he can. "How many times can I do the right thing for the right reason and be hurt because of it?" Only the Lord knows.

To be blunt and metaphorical, each of us plays the cards we're dealt. Wishing for different cards won't help. Comparing our cards to those held by others won't help. We do what we can with what we have right now. And when we do that to God's glory, we discover a certain nobility in even the smallest victories of life.

We love the power of godly support systems—family, friends, and church. An often overlooked aspect of Joseph's faithfulness is that he endured astounding setbacks with no known human support. God was all he had, and God was enough. He's always enough. We prefer not to battle loss and pain alone; we recognize and appreciate the "two are better than one" principle (Eccl 4:9–12). But we love the subtle counterpoint within the story of Joseph. The person who stands with God is never alone.

CAVEATS

We dare not think of Joseph as superhuman. He was a godly, grounded, spiritually-minded young man who chose to honor God no matter his station in life. His God was always bigger than his situation.

The life of Joseph is one of Scripture's strongest statements of the sovereignty of God. Some have unwisely asked, "How could God be fair (just, loving) and let all these things happen to Joseph? There's never a blessing in questioning the goodness of God. God's goodness is a given. We exist by His will and for His glory. Challenging or not, our highest good is His service.

When we face sequential setbacks, there's a far better question than "Why me?" In terms of fairness, we ask, "Why not me?" I have no special status; I'm owed no breaks. In terms of faith, we ask, "What is or what can God teach me through this? How can He draw me toward Him and make me more like Jesus?" In terms of attitude, we ask, "How is God helping me in this moment? In what ways is He with me?" In terms of service, we ask, "What tools is God giving me that I can use to help others? What opportunities to serve exist within this challenge?" And if no clear answers come, we wait, pray, serve, and endure. Rest is coming. Home awaits, but it's not on this earth.

QUESTIONS FOR DISCUSSION

1. How do you explain Joseph's consistent faithfulness during his stunning sequence of setbacks and disappointments?
2. What do you most admire about Joseph? Why?
3. Of all the whams Joseph faced, which do you think most challenging? Why?

4. How did Joseph find the strength to forgive his brothers?

5. Why do most of us see our own setbacks and disappointments as more severe and challenging than the trials faced by others?

WHAM 7: MOSES

LIFE IN A PRESSURE COOKER

THE STORY

Parts of the life of Moses are notably well known to many believers—though separating biblical teachings from Hollywood depictions presents major challenges. He was born under the sentence of death, being a male Hebrew baby in a fearful Egypt (Exod 1). His parents' plan to save his life was brilliant—set him afloat in the reeds near where Pharoah's daughter bathed. Scripture doesn't say that Miriam, his sister, was posted to watch (Exod 2:4). In either case, her concern and curiosity prove to be instruments of God's providence. Pharaoh's daughter saw the ark and sent a servant to get it. As she opened it, the child wept, and she was hooked. Miriam offered to find a Hebrew woman to nurse the child, and Jochebed was paid to care for her son. Only God can tie a bow that neatly! At some point after weaning, Moses was delivered to Pharaoh's daughter and *"became her son" (Exod 2:10)*.

Moses was with his mother long enough to know and appreciate his heritage (Exod 2:11ff). He identified with his people to the degree that he not only checked on their well-being, he defended an oppressed servant to the point of killing the Egyptian who was beating him.

Moses accurately anticipated Pharoah's reaction to the killing so he ran for his life (Exod 2:14–15). Lest we mistake this as an act of cowardice, the next paragraph tells us how Moses defended the seven daughters of the priest of Midian from a band of rude shepherds. That bold act leads to a marriage, a son, and forty years in obscurity —in many ways the easiest part of Moses' life.

Opportunity and complications arose when God called Moses through the famous burning bush (Exod 4). After the Lord overcame his infamous resistance, he returned to Egypt to demand the release of God's people. "Resistance" became a key concept. Pharaoh resisted God's command and the fickle people (Exod 5:15–23) complained and blamed Moses at the first sign of struggle.

Moses learned much about fickleness and complaint. At the Red Sea they accused him of leading them from the safety of slavery to be massacred (Exod 14:11–12). When the drinking water was bitter, they complained (Exod 15:22–24). They complained when food was scarce with the ridiculous words, *"Oh that we had died by the hand of the Lord in Egypt" (Exod 16:1–4)*. Free manna wasn't enough, they complained for lack of meat (Num 11). They again complained for lack of water, and the complaint was increasingly personal. According to Scripture, *"the people quarreled with Moses" (Exod 17:2)*.

Moses faced judicial and administrative pressures as recorded in Exodus 18. People stood before him all day. As much as they complained, they trembled in fear at Sinai (Exod 19:16). On that day we presume that they were happy to have Moses represent them in the mountaintop meeting with God. But when his return from the mountain was perceived as delayed, they rebelled against God and Moses by worshiping the golden calf (Exod 32). In addition were the episodes of Aaron and Miriam's jealousy (Num 12) and the rebellion of Korah (Num 16).

Could any pressure be worse for Moses than the people refusing to trust God and enter the promised land (Num 13–14)? They even proposed choosing a leader to take them back to Egypt. Perhaps there was a greater pressure as recorded in Numbers 14:11–12. God proposed annihilating His chosen people and raising up a new nation with Moses as its father. And so much of this happened as Moses led an ungrateful and struggling nation through hostile desert territory under constant threat of attack from savage pagans.

THE WHAMS

Some of the blows faced by Moses are difficult to describe. At what point was he old enough to understand the dangerous and difficult situation of his birth and earliest years? When he was told the story, how did it impact him?

We don't know the age at which Moses transitioned from his parents' home to the royal court. Clearly, he was old enough to have an established and enduring sense of his identity as a Hebrew. But was that transition a wham —losing direct and daily contact with mom, dad, and siblings—or was it an advancement into opulence, adventure, and the best of educations? Could it be parts of both?

We're certain of the impact of killing the Egyptian. Moses' fear was immediate and life-changing. It was a situation of flee or die. In one event, he went from quasi-royal to criminal, from protected insider to hunted outsider. And the lifestyle adjustment from son of Pharaoh's daughter to shepherd in the wilderness had to be huge.

While we don't condone his excuse-making as God called him to return to Egypt, we certainly understand it. There was a new Pharaoh, but there probably wasn't a statute of limitations on murder. It looked like a suicide mission, and the liberation of his people must have seemed humanly impossible.

Pharoah's opposition to Moses' request was to be expected. We would not say the same of the Hebrews' pounding personal attacks on Moses. They depended on his leadership, but accused him of being a sociopath—his design was to murder them. Their "amnesia" regarding pleas for deliverance is stunning. In their critical retellings, life was never so bad in Egypt. Slavery and oppression had major advantages.

We can't imagine the daily pressure of leading a huge fledgling nation on a defining journey through hostile territory to a land they'd have to take by conquest. As for the unstable nation, perhaps the disappointments of their continual complaining could have been anticipated. Perhaps Moses found ways to steel himself. That's difficult to imagine with the ambush attack by his brother and sister. He was the humblest man on earth (Num 12:3), and his closest family thought the opposite!

Rubbing salt in old wounds, once they completed the exodus and stood on the brink of success, the people balked—they rebelled against God yet again. And it was during their forty years of punishing wilderness wanderings that Moses—in a terrible moment of conflict and frustration—failed to honor God properly and was banned from Canaan (Num 20:12). He saw the promised land, but he died without completing his mission.

IMPLICATIONS

How much pressure can a human bear? Notably more than we tend to think. Metaphorically, we think of most carbon crumbling under pressure while some endures to form diamonds. We think of metal being tempered by fire and pounding to be hardened into higher service. Many have noted that Moses was on the forty-year plan—forty years in Egypt, forty in Midian, and forty leading the exodus. We love the formative implications. We don't see Moses at age 40 being able to cope, endure, and excel like Moses post-eighty. With God's help, we can get better over time.

We present this lesson as Moses facing life in a pressure cooker. While accurate, we dare not underplay the support God gave Moses and the support He gives us. In a sense, Moses survived due to the courageous Hebrew midwives. The love and courage of his parents and his sister played a role. In Jethro and his kin, Moses found a haven and a second family during a major low-point in life. Aaron—like all of us—was flawed, but he helped Moses in countless ways. Eventually there was Joshua, but always there was God. We think of Ephesians 6:10, *"Finally, brethren, be strong in the Lord and in the power of his might."*

Moses reminds us that the daily pressures of life, even the fiercest ones, need not destroy us. It's not about the level, duration, or frequency of pressure; it's about how we choose to cope. There are definite limits to human capacity and endurance. Not so with the Lord. Those who cast every anxiety on Him (1 Pet 5:7) find our God to be *"our refuge and strength, a very present help in trouble" (Ps 46:2)*. We love the emphasis on times of trouble, but He's our very best help every day.

The life of Moses strongly reminds us not to expect life in God's service to be only ease and victory. Biblically and experientially, we know that whams will come. Their exact nature, source, and timing may surprise us. But we should be neither shaken nor surprised that they come. Even the sinless Christ could not avoid the whams of life in a sin-damaged world.

The life of Moses strongly reminds us that sin has consequences even for the best of people. Some view Numbers 20:12–13 as amazingly unfair. *"Moses spends forty-plus years doing virtually everything right, and God cuts him off from Canaan for a single transgression."* No human has the standing to sit in judgment of God. We'd be foolish to assert that this was Moses' only transgression. We'd also be foolish to assert that Canaan was Moses' ultimate goal. We believe with all our hearts that we'll see Moses in heaven (Luke 9:28–36)—everyone's ultimate goal.

CAVEATS

Moses' life was permeated with miracles of God, and we love that. Moses' life was also stunningly blessed by the providence of God as manifested by the courageous midwives, his loving parents, his caring sister, his articulate brother, and his generous and wise father-in-law. If we were tempted to think, "God can't help us like He helped Moses because we live in a post-miraculous age," we'd need to think again. God can still do amazing things without the public suspension of natural laws.

We have proposed that God used the pressures faced by Moses to make him stronger. We have not argued that those who treated Moses unfairly and disrespectfully were blameless because God used their evil actions to bring about good. May we never step into the circular "illogic" of claiming that it's permissible to do wrong so long as the results are good. The devil must love such twisted and unbiblical thinking.

QUESTIONS FOR DISCUSSION

1. What qualified Moses to serve as the leader of the exodus?

2. Of all the pressures that Moses endured, which do you view as the most challenging? Why?

3. Why are certain pressures so challenging to one person but seemingly no big issue to others?

4. How does it help us to remember that God can use the pressures of life to grow, deepen, equip, and refine us?

5. In your judgment, what was the biggest help God gave Moses in facing the pressures of an extra-demanding and complicated life?

WHAM 8: NAOMI

LOST HOPE

THE STORY

The book is called Ruth for good reason, and we don't dispute that. But the second most prominent character in the story, Naomi, merits strong attention, too.

Elimelech, Ruth, and their two sons left Bethlehem for neighboring Moab due to a famine. After Elimelech died, Mahlon and Chilion married, but both of them also died. Naomi heard that the famine was over and decided to return to Judah (Ruth 1:6–7). Her loyal daughters-in-law began the journey with her, but she blessed them and urged them to return to their mothers. Orpah did, and Ruth—famously—did not.

Naomi's return excited the people of Bethlehem, but only briefly. She was not the same lady who left.

> *Do not call me Naomi [pleasant]; call me Mara*
> *[bitter], for the Almighty has dealt very*
> *bitterly with me. I went away full, and the*
> *Lord has brought me back empty. Why call*
> *me Naomi when the Lord has testified*
> *against me and the Almighty has brought*
> *calamity upon me? (Ruth 1:20–21)*

Naomi labeled herself hopeless and defeated. With no husband, no sons, and no heirs, she saw herself without recourse, without joy, and without a meaningful future. In her grief, she could not see the blessing of faithful Ruth. In her grief, she could not see the foreshadowing in her own words. If God indeed is the Almighty, this story isn't over. Because God is the Almighty, even lost hope isn't lost forever.

THE WHAMS

Grief doesn't get better with practice. Every loss is new and unique. The text reports but doesn't discuss the initial loss of their homeland. In Moab Naomi and her family were, at best, foreigners. Perhaps they were refugees, even intruders.

In the loss of her husband, at least she had the comfort of her sons. While that comfort lasted a decade, Ruth 1:5 reads like both sons died within a narrow time. In a notably patriarchal culture, Naomi found herself without a protector—and likely without a way to make a living—in a foreign land.

We can understand the decision to return to Judah, but that involves yet another wham. Whatever friendships and support system she had built in Moab would be lost. It begs the question, "Can a person go home again?" Even if you can—physically, will home still be home? Going home without Elimelech, Mahlon, and Chilion had to be bittersweet at best, and Naomi couldn't find the sweet part.

There's the possibility of another wham, though we've never heard it mentioned. We know the rest of the story—the happy ending, and it flavors our understanding of chapter 1. We celebrate Ruth's love and loyalty, her devotion and determination. We don't know that Naomi thought like that. It's possible, especially in her pain, that Naomi took another view. "Great. I try to do the girls a favor and send them back to their mothers, but Ruth will have none of that. Not only will I have to take care of myself, now I'll be responsible for this young foreigner in a land that's not safe for her." Pain tends to skew thinking in dark directions.

There's a wham of attribution in Naomi's explanation of her name change. *"The Almighty has dealt very bitterly with me … the Lord has brought me back empty,"* and *"the Lord has testified against me, and the Almighty has brought calamity upon me" (Ruth 1:20–21).* By our count, she lays her losses at God's feet four times! The number rises to five if we remember 1:13, *"The hand of the Lord has gone out against me.*" At the best she felt harmed by God. It could have been much worse. She could have felt forsaken, judged, and separated from God. Hope was gone.

IMPLICATIONS

There are major positives within Naomi, even in her darkest hours. Ruth 1:9–13 indicates genuine concern for the well-being of Orpah and Ruth. Her logical case for asking them to stay in Moab is supported by sound reasoning. Naomi gave thought to their plight and did not want to pull them into further sorrow.

Even though Naomi "credited" God with her losses, there's no indication that she stopped believing in or respecting Him. She invokes his name positively: *"May the Lord deal kindly with you as you have dealt with the dead and with me. The Lord grant that you may find rest" (Ruth 1:8–9).* Ruth mentioned Naomi's God so positively as she defended her decision to stay with Naomi, *"... your God shall be my God" (Ruth 1:16–17).*

When hope seemed lost and the situation proved dire, Naomi chose to return to God's country and God's people. We know that God owns all and loves everyone, but in this era, Israel was the chosen nation and they were living in the land that God promised and delivered to them. Perhaps there's a quiet hint of seeing the need to find God again.

We see one more major positive within Ruth 1. Though Naomi tried nobly to get Ruth to go home, once she saw Ruth's determination, she dropped the matter. *"And when Naomi saw that she was determined to go with her, she said no more" (Ruth 1:18).* Regrettably, few people follow Naomi's sound example. When there's nothing else to say, say nothing. Don't nag, grind, rehash, punish, and destroy relationships when all has been said that needs to be said.

THE REST OF THE STORY

Though Naomi declared herself bitter and hopeless, we know the story doesn't end that way. Naomi's emotional and spiritual rebirth is fascinating. There's the tender response when Ruth asked to glean in the barley fields: *"Go, my daughter" (Ruth 2:2).* The language of family is the language of love. Notice how many times the word "daughter" appears in subsequent verses.

Naomi invoked the blessing of the Lord on the landowner who has been kind to Ruth (Ruth 2:19). Her mind turned to thoughts of Ruth's safety (Ruth 2:22) and then to thoughts of her future (Ruth 3:1–5). We'd never view Naomi's unorthodox advice to Ruth as a pattern for others, but it succeeded because it hinged on the reliable and godly character of Boaz, a major compliment to him. We love what we see as Naomi's restored and growing confidence (Ruth 3:6).

And the story ends with all the women celebrating Naomi's triple blessing (Ruth 4:13–16). She has a grandson who is both heir and redeemer, her life and hope have been restored, and she has a daughter-in-law *"who loves [her], who is more to [her] than seven sons."* The blessing moves to fourfold in 4:17 as we note that Obed is great grandfather to King David and ultimately an ancestor of THE King. If we summarized Naomi's life (and ours) in a single sentence, hope is never lost until God says it's lost.

CAVEATS

Like so many other biblical stories, Naomi reminds us that tragic things happen to fine people. Attributing those tragedies directly to God is neither wise not helpful. We're far more blessed to look for God's helping hand and for ways we can help others.

Naomi also reminds us that sometimes our greatest strengths and treasures are under our very noses. They're so close that we fail to see them—especially when we remain focused on our struggles and losses.

The book of Ruth also subtly and strongly warns against xenophobia—the fear of people we view as foreigners. Ruth was a Moabitess—not a member of God's chosen people, but she chose God and honored Him faithfully. And she stands in the lineage of Jesus the Christ.

Naomi experienced a storybook ending—a marriage, a baby, and great joy. We dare not assert that all the faithful will enjoy that outcome. We love the joy, but our hope doesn't lie in this life. Our ultimate joy resides in heaven where hope gives way to eternal life.

QUESTIONS FOR DISCUSSION

1. To the best of our knowledge, God took no offense and offered no correction when Naomi blamed her calamities on Him. Why? What should this teach us?

2. How do you explain the series of severe whams suffered by Naomi? What caused them?

3. Does this lesson overstate Naomi's loss of hope? Give reasons for your answer.

4. List the major turns/factors in God's restoration of Naomi's hope. Which do you find most surprising? Most powerful?

5. Will those who suffer great loss, but don't have a happy ending like Naomi, be harmed by reading her story? How could potential harm be minimized?

WHAM 9: DAVID

LOSING THE MORAL HIGH GROUND

THE STORY

In the briefest of forms, an obscure shepherd, youngest son of his father, is anointed king of Israel and allies with God at a level rewarded with the promise, *"I will establish the throne of his kingdom forever" (2 Sam 7:13)*. This chapter focuses on events recorded in 2 Samuel 11–24, particularly 11–15, where David sinned, tolerated sin, lost the moral high ground within his family, and paid a terrible price.

2 Samuel 11:1 makes clear that King David was in the wrong place. It was *"the time when kings go out to battle,"* but David didn't go. He sent General Joab and the troops, but he remained in Jerusalem. He saw something that a gentleman should not see, a lady bathing. Then, he did what a spiritual man should not do, he inquired about her. He sent for her, sinned against her, and brought the sword into his house forever (2 Sam 12:10–12).

The details are fierce, including the murder of Uriah, Bathsheba's husband (2 Sam 11:6–25). Such could not be done in secret; at the very least, Joab and those to whom he gave the withdrawal orders knew. We wonder whether David's moral shortcomings emboldened Amnon's assault of his sister Tamar. We wonder whether those same failings led David to take no action to punish the rapist (2 Sam 13:21). And we have no wonder that David's failure to act contributed to Absalom's execution of Amnon (2 Sam 13:22–29).

How much did Absalom's violence and subsequent exile contribute to his rebellious attempt to take his father's throne by force? It's part of David's bringing the sword into his own house.

The turmoil and violence didn't stop with the death of Absalom. At a minimum, it continued through the conflict over David's successor. As Adonijah rushed to claim the throne, David moved to crown Solomon as he had promised Bathsheba (1 Kgs 1–2). As the conflict deepened, King Solomon ordered the execution of his brother Adonijah (1 Kgs 2:24–25). Would Adonijah have behaved more wisely had his father offered rebuke and correction? 1 King 1:5–6 strongly implies that he might have. Would David have practiced better parenting had he not lost the moral high ground years before?

THE WHAMS

David suffered many blows outside the scope of this chapter. His brother assumed bad motives and scolded him harshly before he heroically faced Goliath (1 Sam 17:28–29). King Saul, whom he served with respect and loyalty, conspired to have him killed (1 Sam 18:6–9 & 28–29, 19:1 & 10 & 15). On one occasion, David had to pretend to be mad to escape the Philistines (1 Sam 21:10–15). He endured the indignity of having his king give his wife to another man (1 Sam 25:44). He even endured a time when his own soldiers wanted to kill him (1 Sam 30:1–6). His wife harshly condemned him for dancing before the ark (2 Sam 6:20–23). But these whams pale in comparison to the ones within our text.

David sinned against God, the nation, his family, Bathsheba, Uriah, and himself in the adultery with Batheseba. What he did in secret was exposed by God (2 Sam 12:12). We doubt that he had an inkling of the breadth, depth, and severity of Nathan's words, *"The sword shall never depart from your house" (2 Sam 12:10)*. Think of the labels he invited: adulterer, conspirator, murderer, weak father, unjust leader, and weakened king.

David's sinful actions created an avalanche of hits within his family, including the pain and embarrassment of the death of his first son with Bathsheba, incestuous rape, the executions of two of his sons by their brothers, the indignity and danger of Absalom's rebellion, and being mocked in the street by Shimei (2 Sam 16). How much pain could he have avoided by choosing to live more righteously?

IMPLICATIONS

We don't mean to assert above that David could "unsee" or know in advance about Bathsheba's bath time. We see what enters our field of vision, but that's not the whole story. We've always loved the old school truth: "There are some things a gentleman (or a good lady) does not see." He doesn't pause to look, he doesn't dwell on the image, he quickly diverts his attention, and he purposefully upgrades his focus. He doesn't surrender to the temptation; he doesn't give himself permission to inquire or engage. He fights for his soul and his honor then and there. And he prays for God's help.

As with Jacob and Joseph, David faced so many whams. Part of that flowed from his high profile as war hero and king. Part flowed from his long reign, forty years. His public life was even longer. Part flowed from the fact that the Bible tells us far more about David than most characters. Positively, David's ongoing repentance blesses us; he kept turning back to God. Scarily, we see in David the remarkable human ability to be ambushed by sin time after time. They should, but life's whams often don't improve our spiritual eyesight (Prov 22:3 & 27:12).

Among the countless reasons to battle sin is the fact that we can't foresee the devastating effects of our sins on the lives of others. We know *"the wages of sin is death"* *(Rom 6:23)*, but that's just the ultimate payday for those who aren't forgiven. Sin has countless paydays—costs and punishments on us and on innocent people around us—even before we face God's final judgment. And many of those wages aren't erased even by God's forgiveness.

CAVEATS

This lesson focuses on some of David's major failures. We dare not forget that David is not defined by those failures. He didn't rejoice in them. He did not stick and stay in sin. He spoke the beautiful, essential words of 2 Samuel 12:13, *"I have sinned against the Lord."* No doubt he spoke those words and practiced that repentance many times (Ps 51). We'd never make light of sin, but we confidently assert that God is better at forgiving than we are at sinning.

The focus of this chapter is that David damaged his nation, his family, and himself when he surrendered the moral high ground through sin. We believe we have presented biblical truth. But we know this is a truth easily twisted by the devil. He'd love for us to overprocess: "Since we all sin, we have all surrendered the highest of moral standing. Therefore, we have no standing to teach and discipline our children. How can we call them to God's perfection (1 Pet 1:13–15) when we—and they—know our own failings? It's hypocrisy, and everyone hates a hypocrite."

We need more than human thinking at this point. God

did not take the kingdom from David. God didn't lower his standards to accommodate David's failings. God didn't hide David's sin or its consequences. Obviously, God wants us to learn from this sad story.

Even when we sin, we must keep standing and humbly calling for God's best. God can use our examples of penitence and improvement to help others. There's a sense in which "losing the moral high ground" may be overstatement. Such losses need not be total or permanent. We always have the option of turning back to God and doing better (1 John 1:5–10). On a common-sense level, even a weakened voice calling for right living is better than no voice at all. We can't rightly fail to try. Embarrassed silence is not an option,

QUESTIONS FOR DISCUSSION

1. Why is it so easy for humans to trade a moment's pleasure for a lifetime of damage and regret?
2. Rather than a conspiracy that led to multiple killings and civil war, what options for dealing with his adultery were available to David?
3. While the actions of Amnon, Absalom, and Adonijah were their responsibility, to what degree do you see the actions and inactions of David contributing to their respective sins?

4. To what degree can moral high ground be reclaimed once it is lost?

5. By what process can we reclaim moral high ground?

WHAM 10: ELIJAH

PINNACLE TO PIT

THE STORY

It seems an understatement say that Elijah lived dramatically. He lived on the razor's edge, publicly opposing some of the most evil villains within Scripture. He also lived a series of stunning contrasts.

We meet Elijah in 1 Kings 17:1 when God had him tell King Ahab, *"There shall be neither dew nor rain these years, except by my word."* And it didn't rain for three and a half years (Jas 5:17). During much of that time, God had the prophet hide, first at the brook Cherith and later with a widow and her son in Zarephath. During that time, oil and flour in the widow's house miraculously never ran out, and Elijah raised the lady's son from the dead.

1 Kings 18 records what we view as that high point of Elijah's life, the dramatic showdown with 450 prophets of Baal and 400 prophets of Asherah. Before the king and

the nation, a contest ensued. Two altars were built, and a bull was placed on each: *"And the God who answers by fire, he is God."* The dramatic story merits reading in its entirety.

Of course, the true God sent fire—the fake gods couldn't. God's fire consumed even the stones of the altar. The people believed their eyes and declared God to be the Lord. At Elijah's urging, they killed the false prophets. At Elijah's warning, Ahab hurried home before the drought-breaking rain made travel impossible. It's a chapter of stunning odds, stunning theatre, and stunning victory.

In a major sense, the victory was short-lived. Jezebel ordered the death of Elijah (1 Kgs 19:1–2). For a second time, Elijah fled the wrath of Ahab and Jezebel, but this time was different. He fled in fear and despair. He fled of his own volition, not at God's command. And he announced to God his desire to die (1 Kgs 19:4). He fell from pinnacle to pit, believing he alone remained loyal to the Lord (1 Kgs 19:10, 14, & 18).

God's surprising rescue of Elijah was in many ways just as dramatic as the events on Mount Carmel (1 Kgs 19:4–18). Through an angel, God provided food and water, moved him to a safer location, showed him impressive power, and corrected his errant thinking. Then, the Lord commissioned him to anoint two kings and his prophetic successor. God moved him from the pit back to a position of power and service.

Elijah faithfully accepted his recommission. He—again—confronted evil Ahab (1 Kgs 21:17–26). He confronted and rebuked the next king, Ahaziah (2 Kgs 1), even to the point of calling down fire from heaven to destroy more than 100 of his soldiers. Second Kings 2 records Elijah's stunning exit from the earth. The prophet who once prayed to die, never died. He was taken up by God in a whirlwind, riding in a chariot of fire! And even that's not the end of the story as we meet Elijah again during the transfiguration of the Christ (Matt 17:1–13). Elijah remained a powerful positive figure in Jewish thought even in the days of Jesus (Matt 11:17 & 16:14).

THE WHAMS

For some, being told by God to hide from an evil king would have been a blow (1 Kgs 17:3). Being fed by ravens could not have been a joy (1 Kgs 17:6). Neither would depending on the kindness of an impoverished widow. Perhaps the hardest blow from this challenging chapter of Elijah's life would be facing the wrath of that faithful widow when her son died (1 Kgs 17:17–18), though God provided a happy ending.

On a minor level, Elijah endured being called *"troubler of Israel"* by his king (1 Kgs 18:17). We say "minor" because the prophet rightly rejected the false accusation.

The emphatic blow we emphasize in this chapter is the contrast between 1 Kings 18 and 19, from the stunning victory on Mount Carmel to Jezebel's death threat and the subsequent flight into despair. How could Elijah's outlook and attitude pivot so dramatically? How could this pillar of faith who stood one-against-950 suddenly fold and ask God to take his life?

IMPLICATIONS

Psychological explanations of Elijah's collapse often center around depression, suggesting that the adrenaline-laced high point of Mount Carmel naturally led to an equal but opposite depression. Certainly, Elijah's language and action fit depression. Just as certainly, God's treatment of Elijah is what a depressed person would need—rest, food, water, conversation, reasons for hope, improved thinking, addition to his support system (Elisha), and a renewed sense of purpose (anointing kings, participating in God's plan for judgment and justice).

From observation and personal experience, we know that, both spiritually and emotionally, notable lows often follow major highs. We need not prove or embrace a diagnosis of depression to benefit from the warning provided by Elijah. No one is so strong as to be immune from fear, fatigue, or failures of faith. We need not diagnose to be reminded of 1 Corinthains 10:12: *"Therefore let him who thinks he stands take heed lest he fall."* God is the only true rock and refuge. None of us has the personal strength to stand against all this world can throw at us.

Elijah's pinnacle to pit story powerfully reminds us of the power of false beliefs. While Elijah thought, *"I, even I only, am left,"* he was off by 7,000 (1 Kgs 19:18). As surely as the truth sets free (John 8:32), errant thinking and false doctrine limit and imprison. Elijah's error begs us to check our facts before choosing a course of action.

Elijah's story reminds us of our need for community and camaraderie. At least twice, he used the words, *"I, even I only, am left"* (1 Kgs 19:10 & 14). Ironically, Elijah's sense of community and camaraderie worked against him during this episode. *"I am no better than my fathers"* (1 Kgs 19:4). We think of what Elijah might have said in his heart: *"My fathers, the prophets who came before me, also served faithfully. They taught God's truth, they urged repentance, and they failed. What they did made no lasting difference, and they're all dead now."* We think of 1 Kings 18:13, Matthew 23:37, Acts 7:51–53, Romans 11:3, and 1 Thessalonians 2:14–15. Rebellious people killing God's prophets is hardly a minor theme in Scripture.

Elijah's story reminds us of how quickly our circumstances can change. It wouldn't be a stretch to think of Elijah as a national hero at the end of 1 Kings 18. A terrible drought has ended. The people have united to oppose false religion. They have in one voice declared God to be the Lord. It looks for all the world like the dawning of a new day. Could this be the source of Elijah's despair? *"I've stood for God. I've been courageous. I've put my life on the line. And nothing's changed. Ahab and Jezebel still rule. All this, and I'm a dead man walking."*

We dare not so focus on Elijah that we forget to focus on God. God protected Elijah from the rulers of Israel, he protected Elijah from famine, and he protected Elijah from himself. God refused to reject Elijah during the depth of his struggles. In fact, God struggled with and for his prophet, just like He struggles with and for us. God battles for the hearts and souls of those whom He loves. God loves the whole world, and he expects the same from us.

CAVEATS

Did Elijah disappoint God by running away and praying for death after Jezebel's death threat? Though the natural answer is yes, Scripture doesn't comment. We know the weakness of arguments from silence; the Bible can report an event accurately, choose not to record a judgment, and leave the reader to figure things out based on the whole of revelation. God is the master teacher, He made us in His image, and He knows that we learn best when we are heavily invested in the process.

It's possible that the interplay of 1 Kings 18 and 19 is precautionary in multiple ways. Obviously, don't expect even a huge victory to be the end of our war with evil. Evil weakened is not evil destroyed. The devil always has multiple plans of attack. Often our greatest enemy is us.

Consider how we might think of ourselves in the role of Elijah. Wouldn't we love to be such a dynamic and courageous force for good? Wouldn't we love to be put into such a public setting where our faith plays a clear role in defeating evil? Wouldn't we love—just once—to be God's hero? In precautionary terms, we're wise to be careful what we ask for. The distance between pinnacle and pit is terribly short. Public heroes aren't the only kind, likely not even the most numerous kind. There's tremendous wisdom in 1 Timothy 2:2. One reason we pray for those in prominent places—places of authority, is *"that we may live a peaceful and quiet life, godly and dignified in every way."* We love the reason that's given because *"God desires all people to be saved and to come to the knowledge of the truth" (1 Tim 2:4).* We've heard that calm existence described as a life of significant obscurity. It's not about us, our feelings, or our glory. It's always about serving God and bringing souls to him.

QUESTIONS FOR DISCUSSION

1. Is there a danger of over-applying Elijah's story from 1 Kings 18–19? Could his story tempt some to reject the joy of spiritual victories in anticipation of the pits that could follow?

2. Why would the Lord preserve the story for Elijah's struggles? Why tell us about the dark days of such a beloved biblical hero?

3. Why are Christians sometimes tempted to hide their spiritual and emotional struggles, even from other Christians?

4. In what ways does it harm a Christian to hide his or her struggles? In what ways can it help to intelligently share our struggles?

5. How could Satan have used the memory of Elijah's pit of despair to harm him in the future?

WHAM 11: JEREMIAH

WHEN ALL THE WORLD'S AGAINST YOU

THE STORY

Jeremiah stands as one of the most tragic biblical figures. In the broadest overview, he followed Isaiah and overlapped with Ezekiel and Daniel during the catastrophic last days of pre-exilic Judah. He strongly opposed the continued moral and spiritual erosion of his people, knowing that his words went unheeded (Jer 4–5). He endured the three horrific Babylonian invasions of Judea. He was thought by his own people to be both a traitor and a false prophet because he described the invasions as God's just punishment and urged the people not to resist (Jer 28–29 & 38:17–23). Many conclude from Jeremiah 43:1–7 that Jeremiah was involuntarily carried into Egypt by a faithless remnant of the remaining Jews. The pain and weeping recorded within the book of Jeremiah is fierce, only to be followed by the even darker book of Lamentations.

Jeremiah was called by God at a very young age (Jer 1:6–8). Before his call—likely even before his birth—the fate of his nation had been sealed (Isa 39:6–7). Because of sin, the Jews would endure seventy years of Babylonian captivity (Jer 25:11–12). The whole of Judah would fight against Jeremiah at a level where he would need to be *"a fortified city, an iron pillar, and bronze walls against the whole land, against the kings of Judah, its officials, against its priests, and the people of the land" (Jer 1:18)*. Not to say he would have no allies, but those supporters would be stunningly few.

THE WHAMS

Imagine the pain and pressure of being called to a mission of intervention but knowing your efforts would fail. Not even the intercession of Moses and Samuel—if such were possible—could save them (Jer 15:1)! Just and fierce judgment had been decreed by God. Imagine a political climate where telling God's truth looked for all the world like aiding and abetting an oppressive enemy: *"You are deserting to the Chaldeans" (Jer 37:13)*.

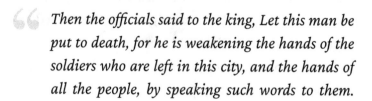

> *Then the officials said to the king, Let this man be put to death, for he is weakening the hands of the soldiers who are left in this city, and the hands of all the people, by speaking such words to them.*

For this man is not seeking the welfare of the people but their harm!" (Jer 38:4)

Imagine the indignity of being beaten by your countrymen and imprisoned for "many days." And that wham was followed by additional imprisonment in a miry dungeon without food (Jer 38:6–9).

Imagine being commissioned to speak God-given oracles against Judah and virtually every surrounding nation (Jer 43–51). Imagine being publicly opposed by prophets who were offering a false but exceedingly popular message:

> *I have broken the yoke of the king of Babylon. Within two years I will bring back to this place all the vessels of the Lord's house which Nebuchadnezzar king of Babylon took away" (Jer 28:2b–3).*

According to the false prophet Hananiah, there would be no seventy-year captivity, no total defeat by Babylon, but rather vindication and restoration.

Imagine being called to a meeting with your king, being urged to speak nothing but truth, but having your words ignored to the harm of the entire nation (Jer 38:14–38). Zedekiah knew what was right, but he lacked the courage to stand on God's truth!

With the known exceptions of Baruch the scribe and courageous Ebed-Melech, Jeremiah—over many years spanning numerous kings and three Babylonian invasions—stood virtually alone as the voice of truth in his nation. Opposed by government leaders, the military, the priests, false prophets, and the bulk of the people, he preached an unwanted, haunting, and accurate message of God's reckoning. And even after the final invasion, those who remained still showed him no respect.

IMPLICATIONS

Like Noah, Jeremiah stands as a powerful example that it's right to do right even when the world around you is crumbling. The Lord wanted to be on record for doing all He could to save Judah. He wanted the world to know that His judgment of His chosen nation was purposeful and just. From a worldly viewpoint, Jeremiah's ministry was utter failure. From a spiritual perspective, however, he faithfully fulfilled the role given him by God.

Like Noah, Jeremiah stands as a clear reminder that a servant of God can do right even if he or she stands virtually alone. With Noah, there's no record of political or social persecution for the message that he preached. But Jeremiah faced the most intense pressure that evil men could bring to bear. Still, he stood firmly. If he did, so can we.

Like Noah, Jeremiah reminds us that truth and faithfulness can't be determined by popularity or headcount. Jeremiah was despised due to his message of doom and destruction. Had polling existed in his day, he would not have registered. Our minds turn to the narrow gate and the upward way: *"those who find it are few" (Matt 7:13–14)*.

Jeremiah's life reminds us that from a human perspective, ministry can seem terribly unfair. The weeping prophet didn't deserve all that he endured. On our better days, we remember that deserving has little to do with reality. To be blunt, in that we all sin, we all deserve death (Rom 3:23 & 6:23). To be mature, serving God is our greatest honor, no matter the cost. And we can always trust God to do more than make things right (2 Cor 4:16–18).

In many respects, Judah's treatment of Jeremiah models the treatment Jesus suffered during His earthly ministry. Think of Isaiah 53:3 and 7: *"He was despised and rejected by men, a man of sorrows and acquainted with grief ... He was oppressed and afflicted ... ."* Think of Pharaoh's opposition to Moses, Saul's persecution of David, and Ahab and Jezebel's threats against Elijah. With no disrespect to Romans 13 and 1 Timothy 2, governments don't have the best record within Scripture.

CAVEATS

Some might wonder about the omission of Isaiah 9:6, *"and the government shall be upon his shoulder,"* from the paragraph likening the government's opposition to Jesus to the oppression suffered by Jeremiah. The omission is purposeful. Isaiah 9:1–7 doesn't deal with ongoing oppression, governmental or otherwise. It's positive and laudatory. It deals with the coming Messiah's breaking both the yoke of burden and the rod of oppression (Isa 9:2–5). It promises (spiritual) restoration of the throne of David with justice and righteousness (Isa 9:7). It promises *"of the increase of his government and peace there will be no end" (Isa 9:7)*. In Isaiah 9, *"the government shall be upon his shoulder"* is not a prediction of persecution. Rather, it's a declaration that God's new order will rest on the might and power of the Wonderful Counselor, Mighty God, Everlasting Father, and Prince of Peace whom God will send.

We'd be wrong to imply that Jeremiah stood on his own strength or character against impossible odds. God knew what was coming from before the beginning. To his credit, Jeremiah chose faithfulness, but it was the Lord who ordered him to prepare himself and made him strong (Jer 1:17–18). It was the Lord who promised from the beginning, *"They will fight against you, but they will not prevail against you, for I am with you declares the Lord, to deliver you" (Jer 1:19)*. Spiritually speaking, we have that same promise (Rom 8, 1 Cor 15). Like us, Jeremiah knew the positive end of the story, but he had no way to grasp how challenging the journey would be.

QUESTIONS FOR DISCUSSION

1. In your judgment, why didn't the Lord give Jeremiah a larger team of coworkers? Why did

God let Jeremiah do so much of his work
alone?

2. What kept Jeremiah from buckling under the
massive pressure that he faced?

3. Can people learn to resist social, religious, and
political pressure? If so, how? (Rom 12:1–2,
John 12:42–43)

4. What should we learn from Jeremiah when we
find ourselves facing thankless, unpopular, or
seemingly impossible tasks?

5. Some could assert that God was unfair to
Jeremiah, giving him a job he never wanted
and having him preach to a doomed people.
How should such a charge be answered? How
could biblical answers to this charge help us?

WHAM 12: DANIEL
STUNNING DISPROPORTION

THE STORY

There are often costs to being among the brightest and best. Daniel and his peers were among those *"of the royal family and the nobility, youths without blemish, of good appearance and skillful in all wisdom, understanding learning, and competent to stand in the king's palace"* taken to Babylon after the first invasion of Judea (Dan 1:4).

Daniel and his friends were taken from Judea to Babylon at the king's command by *"his chief eunuch"* *(Dan 1:3)*. Please forgive the indelicacy of reporting that neutering males from conquered nations was a common practice in the ancient Near East. Presumably, these altered servants wouldn't be distracted by marriage, children, or sexual desire. Their daily lives and their futures would revolve around their work. Some scholars have argued that the range of meaning of the word "eunuch" does not necessarily have surgical implications. Even if that's true, by far the usual meaning is a surgically-altered male. Why would we care? If Daniel, at very young age, involuntarily lost the ability to father children, that alone is an egregious life-altering event. On top of that, he was taken as a captive to serve the nation that attacked—and kept attacking—his homeland.

Daniel endured a series of tests in Babylon. The first concerned Jewish dietary law. In a powerless position in a pagan land, would he "go along to get along" and forget God's word (Dan 1:18–21)? Famously, faithfully, and diplomatically, Daniel and his friends requested permission not to defile themselves. And God blessed them with favor in the palace.

Daniel's next huge test was a death sentence over the failure of the kingdom's wise men to describe Nebuchadnezzar's dream and offer an interpretation (Dan 2). Daniel and his friends respectfully requested time for prayer, and God delivered them.

Daniel's next personal test also involved a dream (Dan 4). The interpretation was that King Nebuchadnezzar would spend *"seven periods of time"*—we're not certain if years, months or weeks—*"with the beasts of the field ... eating grass like an ox."*

As we read Daniel 5, years have passed, Nebuchadnezzar is dead, and Daniel had been forgotten. When the famous hand writes on the wall and no one could read the words, the queen—likely the queen mother—remembered Daniel. He read and interpreted the message of doom. The Babylonian Empire was no more.

Daniel 6 occurs in Daniel's old age. He had again risen to prominence—but this time within the Medo-Persian empire. As King Darius *"planned to set him over the whole kingdom" (Dan 6:1–3)*, his jealous rivals realized: *"We shall not find any ground for complaint against this Daniel unless we find it in connection with the law of his God" (Dan 6:5)*. What a compliment!

Daniel's critics conned the king into enacting a foolish law, and Daniel refused to abide by it. Under threat of death, he prayed from his upper room with widows open as was his longstanding practice. The king looked for opportunity to rescue his faithful servant but could not find a way. God famously intervened to stop the mouths of the lions until Daniel's accusers took his place in the lions' den.

THE WHAMS

We've offered quite a list so far: surgically neutered, torn from his homeland, involuntarily forced to serve the king who destroyed his homeland, pressured to defile his conscience, and unfairly threatened with death. Then, after a stellar career in civil service, he was forgotten. Once remembered, he was plotted against by his fellow leaders and again faced potential death.

Not mentioned above is the pain Daniel felt when he remembered the words we know as Jeremiah 25:12. *"I,*

Daniel, perceived in the books the number of years that, according to the word of the Lord to Jeremiah the prophet, must pass before the end of desolations of Jerusalem, namely, seventy years" (Dan 9:2). As the completion of the seventy years approached, Daniel saw no movement toward the end of the exile. He utterly trusted God and prayed in the most penitent and faithful language. But the wham is clear: "Lord, I know you're good to Your word, but I need help. May I remind you of the prophecy, and ask for understanding? I know our punishment is just, but I ask for deliverance anyway." And God respected him so much that He sent an angel with comfort and answers.

The wham we emphasize in this chapter is the stunningly disproportionate set of losses righteous Daniel suffered due to the sins of his nation. Forces he neither welcomed nor supported destroyed the world as he knew it.

IMPLICATIONS

Daniel teaches us that faith and character are not determined by what happens to us. So much in life is beyond our control. Faith is a choice to trust and obey God. Both character and hope are molded by endurance in the face of suffering (Rom 5:3–4).

We take heart in the absence of any hint that Daniel wasted time and energy asking, "Why me?" or complaining, "Lord, this is stunningly unfair!" We love the fact that Daniel never surrendered his identity as a servant of God.

During trial after trail, he did all that he could to glorify God and serve faithfully.

Daniel is a strong example of the truth that the circumstances of life don't control us. Even the fiercest of events can't keep us from praying and trusting God. In no way do we mean to imply that this is easy—to the best of our knowledge there was nothing easy in Daniel's life once the Babylonians came. There was nothing easy, but there was much that was blessed, wise, and right.

Daniel stands as one of the best biblical examples of commitment to prayer. He and his friends sought God's mercies regarding Nebuchadnezzar's quasi-forgotten dream (Dan 2:15–18). He was steadfast in more-than-daily prayer (Dan 6:10). Prayer meant more to him than life itself. His prayer in Daniel 9 invoked a visit from the angel Gabriel (Dan 9:20–23). Could God have expressed higher respect for a servant's prayer?

Daniel also shows us that servants of God don't really retire. After Nebuchadnezzar died, Daniel seemed to disappear, only to be recalled to service by reading the writing on the wall. God wasn't done with Daniel, and Daniel never balked at God's call.

CAVEATS

Some are greatly troubled over the absence of Daniel in Daniel 3. "Where was Daniel? Did he bow to the golden image?" Bluntly, we don't know where Daniel was, but we know he was separated to some degree from Shadrach,

Meshach, and Abednego at the end of Daniel 2. Chapters 1 and 2 make clear that Daniel was not alone among the Hebrew captives who stand as heroes of faithfulness. We also know that bowing before that idol would be counter to everything we know about Daniel. We're unwise to speculate or borrow trouble. In this case, the absence of information communicates virtually nothing. Daniel 3 reminds us that faithfulness to God is essential even in the face of death and that the faithfulness of Daniel's friends did not depend on Daniel's physical presence. Their trust was in God, not Daniel.

The situation of Daniel's being a eunuch is at best indelicate. To its credit, the Bible never shies away from uncomfortable truth. The Ethiopian treasurer of Acts 8 was no less a seeker, an excellent example, and a potential evangelist because he was also a eunuch. The new convert from Acts 8 isn't the first Ethiopian eunuch within Scripture. Heroic Ebed-Melech who rescued Jeremiah from almost certain death was the first (Jer 38:7–13). Each of these examples urge us to consider the questions: "What makes a man a man?" and "How does God's view of a man differ from the world's view?"

While we find great joy in God's deliverance of Daniel from the lions, we know that caution and wisdom are needed. Daniel would have been just as faithful and just as right had the lions consumed him. We'd never argue that John the Baptizer, James, brother of John, or Stephen were wronged by God because He allowed them to be martyred. From God's perspective, he welcomed each of them to His eternal home as a permanent example of faith and victory. For those tempted to accuse God of unfairness, no human has the wisdom or standing to accuse God.

QUESTIONS FOR DISCUSSION

1. What does Daniel's courage tell us about biblical manhood?

2. What does Daniel's life tell us about the power of faith in the face of potentially crushing circumstances?

3. How did Daniel know how to act and talk so effectively amid dangers and threats of death? How could such a young man have such wisdom?

4. Why would the Lord record Daniel's stellar conduct both as a very young man and again as a graybeard? Why document his faithfulness at both ends of life?

5. Do you think Daniel ever asked himself, "What if? What if I could have had a normal life? What if I hadn't lived in such warring and barbaric times?" Would such questions have blessed him? Harmed him? If so, how?

WHAM 13: ESTHER
ILLUSION OF SAFETY

THE STORY

The book of Esther opens with the odd and challenging story of how virtuous Queen Vashti opened the door for Esther's rise to fame (Esth 1). Though some assert otherwise, we believe Vashti lost her royal place because she refused to be ogled by an assembly of drunken men. Since a new queen was needed, a young beautiful woman was sought. Esther was among those gathered in the harem at Susa for a year of beautifying (Esth 2:1–4 & 12).

Esther—also known as Hadassah—was a Jewess; the descendant of a family that was brought to Persia during one of Nebuchadnezzar's invasions of Judea (Esth 2:5–7). When her parents died, her cousin Mordecai *"took her as his own daughter."* Esther and Mordecai shared an exemplary relationship of trust and respect. Upon Mordecai's instruction, Esther told no one she was Jewish.

By being pleasant and respectful, Eshter earned the favor of Hegai, who had custody of the women. Esther won favor *"in the eyes of all who saw her"*—including the king (Esth 2:15–17). She was proclaimed queen during a great feast. What an amazing rags—and refugee—to-riches story!

As the subtitle of this chapter hints, Esther's story doesn't end at this point of safety and security. Evil Haman hated her cousin Mordecai. His hatred ran so deep that he hatched a plot to murder every Jew in the kingdom (Esth 3). Mordecai famously sought Esther's help in foiling Haman's plan (Esth 4:9–14). But as you may already know, choosing to intervene would put Esther's life at risk (Esth 4:11).

Risking her life, Esther intervened (Esth 5). In a brilliant and skillfully executed plan, she told the king of Haman's evil (Esth 6–7). Exposed and defenseless, Haman was hanged on the very gallows that he built to kill Mordecai. Through all these events, God's providential hand was evident.

Even after Haman was dead, the danger wasn't over. Within the Persian legal system, a decree sealed by the king's ring could not be revoked (Esth 8:8). But there was a solution. A new decree was issued allowing the Jews to defend themselves. Mordecai and Queen Esther led their people in that successful defense, and the feast of Purim was initiated to celebrate God's salvation. Like Daniel, Mordecai was promoted to second-in-the-kingdom (Esth 10:3).

THE WHAMS

No one could assert that Esther lived a trouble-free life. She was an orphan and a resident of a land that included a powerful element who strongly hated Jews. From one perspective, even her beauty worked against her; she was added to the king's harem. Romantically, we tend to see elevation from commoner to queen as a huge promotion. Realistically, we know that royal life exists in a fishbowl with stunning expectations. It may not have been as trouble-free and glamourous as often portrayed by Hollywood. And she lived with the pressure of concealing her ethnicity. One could also see a sharpness in Mordecai's words to her (Esth 4:13–14).

The blow emphasized in this chapter is the way that Esther's initial victory and elevation were shattered by Haman. Even as Esther could have thanked God for her advancement and begun to enjoy her enhanced influence and security, forces were powerfully and secretly at work to endanger her life.

IMPLICATIONS

Esther is a wonderful example of God's power to elevate people to roles of service. Who but God would make an orphan, a refugee, and a foreigner the next queen? We remember Jesus's famous statement: *"But many who are first will be last, and the last first"* (Matt 19:30, 20:16). God can put us exactly where we need to be.

Esther vividly portrays the power of relationships to enhance service and shape destinies. Would young Esther have survived without Mordecai's kindness? Would she have been chosen queen had her ethnicity been known? To what degree did her love and respect for Mordecai help her find the courage to risk her life for the sake of her people? Who could miss the multiple ironies of how God used the Haman/Mordecai conflict to empower His people in a foreign land?

The story of Esther offers a clinic in the depth and power of God's providence. If we employ the metaphor of a chessboard, God moved the Vashti piece using the fear of powerful men to create the need for a new queen. He used Mordecai's wisdom and Esther's respect to conceal Esther's Jewishness. He used Esther's beauty and excellent attitude to win the king's favor. He used Mordecai's intervention to stop an assassination to elevate him and to bring the conflict with Haman to a boil. There's no suspension of natural law (miracle) in these actions, but too much happened in perfect order and with amazing timing to doubt God's guidance of the process.

The book of Esther reminds us that we can be totally unaware of the dangers that surround us. That lack of awareness can be willful, as in Jeremiah's day: *"They have healed the wound of my people lightly, saying 'Peace, peace' when there is no peace" (Jer 8:11).* As in Esther's case, unawareness can be due to events or plots not yet known to us. Whatever the cause, God works to help us stay both "*sober-minded and watchful*" (*1 Pet 5:8*) because human dangers are not the only ones we face (Eph 6:10–12, Job 1).

The Jews' escape from Haman's wicked plot offers one additional reminder; God often allows us a role in our deliverance (Esth 8–10, esp. 8:11. Think of the conquest of Canaan and the book of Judges). From the legal action of a second set of decrees to taking up arms in self-defense, Mordecai, Esther, and the other Jews were not passive observers of God's salvation. God allowed them the blessing and empowerment of playing an active role.

CAVEATS

Mordecai's disrespect for Haman is a challenging aspect of the book of Esther. Upon promoting Haman to second in the kingdom, Ahasuerus commanded everyone to bow down and pay homage to Haman (Esth 3:1–6). Mordecai refused. Lest we miss the point, the text tells us that the king's servants asked Mordecai, "*Why do you transgress the king's command?*" *(Esth 3:3)* No answer was given.

Bible students have long noticed that Mordecai's actions stand in stark contrast to Daniel's respect for both Babylonian and Persian rulers. His conduct was not in keeping with the—admittedly much later—commands of Romans 13, 1 Timothy 2:1–2, or 1 Peter 2:13–17. It doesn't fit Paul's attitude or words from Acts 23:1–5. We offer two observations. First, the Bible is brief and doesn't fully address our every curiosity. Second, it is possible that Mordecai was acting on a command of God that is unknown to us. As noted above, we know the result of Mordecai's approach and God's use of that result.

Some are troubled by the process through which Esther was chosen as queen. She was chosen initially based on physical appearance, she was added to the king's harem, and after a year, she faced a "one night audition" with the king (Esth 2:1–4 & 12–18). Had she not been chosen queen, she would have been considered a concubine, hardly the pattern for marriage from Genesis 2!

We're reminded that Scripture sometimes presents the factual accounts without—in the same text—reminding us that those events lie outside God's will. We know from Genesis 2:24 that God's plan is one man married to one woman for life. We also know that Scripture doesn't directly condemn Jacob, David, and others for having multiple wives. The Lord knows we have both the ability and the responsibility to connect the dots and know right from wrong. Even in texts where sin receives no direct condemnation, the stories often include painful and far reaching consequences of disregarding God's will.

There's a second issue here. How could Esther participate in such a sequence of events and still be righteous? To answer a question with a question, what choice did she have? Other than taking her own life—an action that presents huge problems—what could she have done? To the best of our knowledge, she had no power to refuse. Is her situation somewhat like Joseph serving Pharaoh or Daniel serving the Babylonian and Persian Empires? We think of it somewhat like paying Roman taxes in the time of Jesus—taxes that supported idol worship, gladiatorial games, and an occupying army. God in his grace does not judge us for what we can't control. We think it dangerous and unwise to judge Esther when Scripture does not.

QUESTIONS FOR DISCUSSION

1. Do you see Vashti's actions in Esther 1 as principled or rebellious? Why?
2. At what point do you think Esther realized her adventures were part of something much bigger than herself?
3. Why is the concept of God's providence so challenging for many believers?
4. Does this chapter overstate the issue of Esther's greatest danger coming after she reached a status of safety and security?
5. How should we understand Mordecai's rather stout words to Esther (Esth 4:13–14)? Was he warning her, scolding her, or encouraging her? Is a combination of these motives possible?

SCRIPTURE INDEX

Old Testament

Genesis

1:16	xiii	6:6	8
1:31	xiii	6:8	8
2	93	6:9	8
2:17	1	6:22	8
2:24	6, 93	8:20	9
3	1	8:21–23	9
3:1	xiii	9	11–13
3:1–7	4	9:20–27	9–11
3:7	2	9:24	10
3:15	26	9:28	12
3:16	3	11:27	23
3:16–19	xiii	11:30	23
3:18	2	11:32	24
3:21	5	12	25
4	3	12:1	23
4:1	5	12:4	23
4:25	5	12:10–13	26
6:3	8	13:1–13	25
6:5	8	13:16	25
		14	25
		15	25

16	25	37:4	37
17	25–26	37:5–11	37
17:17	26	37:18–28	37
18:11	25	37:29–36	31–32
18:11–15	26	39	37
18:15	26	39:9	38
20	25	40:1–41:1	38
20:1–13	26	41:51	39
20:10–11	25	41:52	39
21	25	42	38
21:5	23	42:9	38
22	28	50:5	31
22:6	29	50:15	39
24:1–10	28	**Exodus**	
25	30	1	44
25:19–26	34	2:4	44
25:23	35	2:10	45
25:29–34	31	2:11ff	45
25:34	33	2:14–15	45
27	30–31	4	45
27:41	32	5:15–23	45
28:10–17	30	14:11–12	45
28:20–22	34	15:22–24	45
29	31	16:1–4	45
29:13–30	32	17:2	46
29:15–30	30	19:16	46
31:34	31	32	46
32:13–32	30	**Leviticus**	
32:22–32	33	18:21	28
34	34	20:1–5	28
37:2	37		
37:3	31		

Numbers

11	46
12	46
12:3	48
13–14	46
14:11–12	46
16	46
20:12	48
20:12–13	50
32:23	32

Deuteronomy

6:4–5	12
6:13	12
12:31	28

Ruth

1	55
1:6–7	52
1:8–9	55
1:9–13	55
1:13	54–55
1:16–17	55
1:18	56
1:20–21	53–54
2:2	56
2:19	56
2:22	56
3:1–5	56
3:6	56
4:13–16	56
4:17	57

1 Samuel

8	6
17:28–29	61
18:6–9	61
18:28–29	61
19:1	61
19:10	61
19:15	61
21:10–15	61
25:44	61
30:1–6	61

2 Samuel

6:20–23	61
7:13	59
11–24	59
11–15	59
11:1	59
11:6–25	60
12:10	61
12:10–12	59
12:12	61
12:13	63
13:21	60
13:22–29	60
16	62

1 Kings

1–2	60
1:5–6	60
2:24–25	60
11:3–4	6
17:1	66

17:3	68	4:11	89
17:6	68	4:13–14	90, 94
17:17–18	68	5	89
18	66, 68, 70–71	6–7	89
18–19	72	8–10	92
18:13	70	8:8	89
18:17	68	8:11	92
19	68, 71	10:3	89
19:1–2	67	**Job**	
19:4	67, 70	1	92
19:4–18	67	1:1–3	15
19:10	67, 70	1:8	18
19:14	67, 70	1:13–17	17
19:18	67, 69	1:22	17–18
21:17–26	67	2:7	17
2 Kings		2:9	17
1	68	2:11–13	17
2	68	3	16
20–21	6	3:18–19	17
23:10	28	4:7	15
Esther		6	16
1	88	6:24–30	16
2:1–4	88, 93	13:15	19
2:5–7	88	13:15a	20
2:12	88	23:2–7	16
2:12–18	93	3:9–15	17
2:15–17	89	30:20–21	16, 18
3	89	38:1–42:6	17
3:1–6	92	42	19
3:3	92	42:12	22
4:9–14	89	42:17	22

Psalms

46:2	49
51	63

Proverbs

13:15	35
16:25	4
20:1	10
22:3	62
23:29–35	10
27:12	62

Ecclesiastes

3:17–20	xiii
4:9–12	41

Isaiah

9	79
9:1–7	78
9:2–5	79
9:6	78
9:7	79
38	6
39:6–7	75
53:3	78
53:7	78
55:8–9	20

Jeremiah

1:6–8	75
1:17–18	79
1:18	75
1:19	79
4–5	74

8:11	91
15:1	75
19:5	28
25:11–12	75
28–29	74
28:2b–3	76
25:12	83
32:35	28
37:13	75
38	6
38:4	75–76
38:6–9	76
38:7–13	86
38:14–38	76
38:17–23	74
43–51	76
43:1–7	74

Ezekiel

14	13
14:12–20	9

Daniel

1	86
1:3	81
1:4	81
1:18–21	82
2	82, 86
2:15–18	85
3	85–86
4	82
5	82
6	82

6:1–3	83
6:5	83
6:10	85
9	85
9:2	83–84
9:20–23	85

Hosea

14:9	35

New Testament

Matthew

4:10	12
7:13–14	78
11:17	68
16:14	68
17:1–13	68
19:30	90
20:16	90
23:37	70

Luke

2	26
4:13	11
9:28–36	50
12:15b	18

John

1:1–13	6
8:32	70
12:42–43	80
16:12–13	20

Acts

7:51–53	70
8	86
18:26	18
23:1–5	92

Romans

3:23	13, 78
5:1–5	27
5:3–4	84
6:23	33, 63, 78
8	79
8:28	xiv
11:3	70
11:32–33	20
12:1–2	80
12:2	35
12:3	4
13	78, 92

1 Corinthians

10:12	4, 69
15	79

2 Corinthians

4:16–18	78

Galatians

4:4	26
5:21	10
6:7–8	32

Ephesians

6:10	49
6:10–12	92
6:11–12	4

Philippians

4:8	35

Colossians

3:1	35

1 Thessalonians

2:14–15	70

1 Timothy

2	78
2:1–2	92
2:2	72
2:4	72

Hebrews

3:12–19	6
6:4–8	6
11	13, 27
11:7	9
11:13	24
11:19	29

James

1:12–16	34
1:13	4
3:5	12
4:10	21
5:17	66

1 Peter

1:13–15	63
2:13–17	92
3	27
5	13

5:7	49
5:8	11, 18, 92

2 Peter

2:5	9
2:18–22	6
3:8–9	26

1 John

1:5–10	64

Revelation

2:4–5	6

ACKNOWLEDGMENTS

We enjoy working with and through Heritage Christian University Press. We're repeatedly offered outstanding help—and shown amazing patience. Executive Director Jamie Cox continues to refine her layout and typesetting skills. Brittany Vander Mass collaborates with Laura to create covers that are both meaningful and inviting. We also appreciate the marketing efforts of the team at HCU. Their talents improve our endeavors to help others.

We express appreciation to Debbie May and Andy Kizer for their kind endorsements. We thank Andy for going the second mile for his proofreading expertise.

ABOUT THE AUTHORS

Bill Bagents earned his master's degree in counselor education from Auburn University and doctor of ministry from Amridge University. He is currently professor of ministry, counseling, and biblical studies with Heritage Christian University. He has served as an elder, deacon, and minister. Bill has worked as a counselor with the Alpha Center in Florence; he has also done mission work in Albania, Bangladesh, Jamaica, Namibia, Nigeria, the Philippines, Russia and South Africa.

Laura Lynn Stegall Bagents is a career classroom teacher with Florence City Schools. She earned degrees from Auburn University, the University of North Alabama, and the University of Alabama (EdD 2008). Her church-related teaching has included children's Bible classes in local congregations as well as adjunct roles with Heritage Christian University and classes for ladies and children in Albania and on the Western Cape of South Africa.

ALSO BY BILL BAGENTS

Wham! Facing Life's Heavy Hits: Thirteen Old Testament Encounters

by Bill Bagents and Laura S. Bagents

Corrupt Communication: Myths that Target Church Leaders

by Bill Bagents and Laura S. Bagents

Always Near: Listening for Lessons from God

by Bill Bagents

Revisiting Life's Oases: Soul-Soothing Stories

by Bill Bagents

Welcoming God's Word: Reading with Head and Heart

by Bill Bagents

Counseling for Church Leaders: A Practical Guide

by Bill Bagents and Rosemary Snodgrass

Easing Life's Hurts 2nd ed.

by Jack Wilhelm and Bill Bagents

Equipping the Saints: A Practical Study of Ephesians 4:11–16

by Bill Bagents and Cory Collins

HERITAGE
CHRISTIAN UNIVERSITY
PRESS

CYPRESS

To see full catalog of Heritage Christian University Press
and its imprint Cypress Publications, visit
www.hcu.edu/publications